GEOPOLITICS AND GLOBALIZATION
IN THE TWENTIETH CENTURY

GLOBALITIES

Series editor: Jeremy Black

GLOBALITIES is a series which reinterprets world history in a
concise yet thoughtful way, looking at major issues over large
time-spans and political spaces; such issues can be political,
ecological, scientific, technological or intellectual. Rather than
adopting a narrow chronological or geographical approach,
books in the series are conceptual in focus yet present an array of
historical data to justify their arguments. They often involve a
multi-disciplinary approach, juxtaposing different subject-areas
such as economics and religion or literature and politics.

In the same series

Why Wars Happen
Jeremy Black

A History of Language
Steven Roger Fischer

Monarchies 1000–2000
W. M. Spellman

*The Nemesis of Power:
A History of International
Relations Theories*
Harald Kleinschmidt

Geopolitics and Globalization in the Twentieth Century

BRIAN W. BLOUET

To Ed
With warmest regards

Brian Blouet
May 10th, 2001

REAKTION BOOKS

Published by Reaktion Books Ltd
79 Farringdon Road, London EC1M 3JU, UK

www.reaktionbooks.co.uk

First published 2001

Printed and bound in Great Britain by
Cromwell Press, Trowbridge, Wiltshire

British Library Cataloguing in Publication Data

Blouet, Brian W., 1936–
    Geopolitics and globalization in the twentieth century. –
    (Globalities)
    1. Geopolitics 2. Globalization
    I. Title
    320.1'2

ISBN 1 86189 085 0

Contents

Introduction

This book looks at the struggle between the processes of globalization and geopolitical forces over the last century and a half. Globalization is the opening of national space to the free flow of goods, capital and ideas. Globalization removes obstructions to movement and creates conditions in which international trade in goods and services can expand.

Geopolitical policies seek to establish national or imperial control over space and the resources, routeways, industrial capacity and population the territory contains. This definition of geopolitics is in the tradition of German *Geopolitik*, which has its roots in the writings of Freidrich Ratzel[1] in the late nineteenth century.[2] The definition describes the activity of many states through the end of the Cold War.

The game board for globalization is marked out in the territory of sovereign states and no country can move to policies of globalization in isolation. Complete globalization would involve all countries accepting free movement and common standards for many goods, services, and practices, including environmental issues. States have promoted aspects of globalization. Britain, for example, in the second half of the nineteenth century, adopted free trade policies and insisted upon freedom of navigation outside territorial waters – the three-mile limit. The British empire also had a strategic, geopolitical structure with a string of naval bases to put down piracy and ensure freedom of the seas.[3]

The United States now promotes free trade, opening up parts of the vast home market to encourage other states to do the same. The US wants the free movement of goods, capital, ideas, and the worldwide acceptance of laws dealing with copyright, intellectual property, patents and illegal flows of money, drugs, and goods. When threatened by geopolitical states the

US will respond in kind. Cuba remains cut off from the US after allowing the Soviet Union to construct missile bases on the island in 1962. When Iraq invaded Kuwait the US provided the bulk of the forces needed to reverse Iraqi occupation and prevent the regime pursuing expansionist, geopolitical policies in the Persian Gulf.

Tightly controlled geopolitical states of recent history include Nazi Germany, the Soviet Union, Communist China, and North Korea. Nazi Germany and the Stalinist USSR wanted to strictly control national territory and the people living within it. Policy was directed at creating states that were largely self-sufficient (autarkic) and not dependent upon imports of resources or equipment. Both Germany and the Soviet Union had territorial ambitions. Hitler's expansion policies were driven by a desire to acquire more farmland, mineral resources, and timber. Stalin wanted back the non-Russian lands the Tsars had lost earlier in the twentieth century. With those lands came seaports and strategic territory in the Baltic and the North Pacific. Hitler and then Stalin wanted to dominate Eurasia. Britain, the US, and their allies resisted that challenge in the Second World War and the Cold War. The present phase of globalization springs from US actions and policies adopted immediately after the Second World War which undermined the protectionism that had been strengthened by the US and other states in the slump of the 1930s.

GEOPOLITICS AT THE END OF THE NINETEENTH CENTURY

A century ago, earth space was divided into competing empires and spheres of influence. Geopolitical analysts examined the value of segments of earth space and the consequences of powers gaining or losing control of territory. Empires could only gain advantage by taking assets from other imperial systems.

The last third of the nineteenth century was a period of unprecedented technological development and economic growth. The earth was shrinking in terms of the time it took to move people and goods from one region to another. International trade was growing. Large, faster ships reduced the costs of transportation. An observer at any major British port would have seen natural products arriving from all over the world. The prairies and plains of North America, settled by European migrants, were exporting cheap grains to Britain – bad news for wheat growers in Britain but bringing the cost of food down for the majority of people who now lived and worked in cities. On-board refrigeration allowed beef and mutton to be brought from the pampas of Argentina and the grasslands of Australia and New Zealand. Bananas and other tropical fruits came from the Caribbean, and Brazil, in the hinterland of São Paulo, had become a major producer of cheap coffee, exported through Santos. The new globalizing economy was reflected in cities like Chicago and Buenos Aires. Chicago, on the southern shore of Lake Michigan, had grown to be a railroad hub and centre of commodity dealings – grains, hogs, and cattle. The world price of many agricultural products was set in the city on the commodities market.

At mid-century Buenos Aires was still a small provincial capital – the former seat of the viceroyalty of the Rio de la Plata. By the end of the century railroads linked the farms and *estancias* of the pampas to the port of Buenos Aires and exports of grains, livestock, beef, mutton, wool, and hides brought prosperity. Capital was flowing into harbour works, meat-processing plants, utilities, and factories to produce consumer goods. The old colonial streets, near the centre of the city, were redeveloped with elegant buildings and smart shopping streets, linked to the suburbs by electric trams and suburban railways. The *porteños* flattered themselves with talk of their city as the Paris of South America but the central city was a modern place and living standards exceeded those of many European countries, although the wealth was concentrated in the hands of those who held land and political power.

Many observers, in Europe and elsewhere, saw class conflict as a rising cause of trouble. Mass political parties were beginning to emerge. But it was not to be mass political movements, nor ideological differences between states, that moved countries towards the First World War. Wars came, as the world opened up, because governments became greedier for a larger share of earth space. The perceived necessity to control territory led ministers to risk war in order to promote national ambitions in contested space.

Back in 1873 Jules Verne had sent Phileas Fogg *Around the World in Eighty Days*. Verne described a world being integrated by technology. Using everything from horse-drawn cabs to balloons, railroads, steamships and elephants, Fogg made his way around the world, travelling eastward, in time to win his bet. Had Fogg made another journey 30 years later, at the beginning of the twentieth century, faster steamships would have cut transoceanic voyage times in half, cars would have been replacing horse-drawn cabs, electric trams were in the streets of all major cities, buildings were illuminated by electric lights, and Fogg could not only have sent a telegram but he could now have spoken on the telephone. Late in 1903 a motor-powered plane flew successfully.

Around the World in Eighty Days was written at the end of the era of unification. The US had fought a civil war to prevent states leaving the union. Japan, with the Meiji restoration of 1868, created a strong central government with authority over the Japanese archipelago. Italy unified in the 1860s, as did Germany, culminating in the creation of the German empire (1871) at the end of the Franco-Prussian war.

In the wake of unification a sense grew that larger states, integrated by railways and telegraphs, would emerge to control affairs. Speaking to undergraduates at the University of Cambridge in 1882, Professor Seeley put it this way:

> Now if it be true that a larger type of state than any hitherto known is springing up in the world, is not this a serious consideration for those states which rise only to the old level of magnitude? Russia already presses somewhat heavily on central Europe: what will she do when with her vast territory and population she equals Germany in intelligence and organization, when all her railways are made, her people educated, and her government settled on a solid basis – and let us remember that if we allow her half a century to make such progress her population will at the end of that time be not eighty but nearly 160 million. At that time which many present may live to see, Russia and the United States will surpass in power the states now called great.[4]

Darwinian thinking was taking hold.[5] Many policy-makers believed there would be a competition between states from which only the fittest would emerge as powerful players in international relations. Small states were vulnerable and big states, with large resource bases, were more potent.

The emergence of larger states, new boundaries in the Balkans, the scramble for Africa, and the chipping off of territory from the Ottoman empire created a climate in which there was an expectation that boundaries would change. The world was going to be rearranged in terms of sovereign space. The more powerful players would win; the weaker states, like China, would lose. Major world regions – pan regions – would emerge dominated by superstates.[6] Commentators tried to predict the superstates – the US in the Western hemisphere, the British empire (possibly federated) and the Russian empire were on most lists. Germany was determined to be a superstate but would that status come at the expense of France and the empires of Austria-Hungary and Russia? The French saw the rise of Germany as a continuing threat. Austria-Hungary competed uneasily with Russia in the Balkans and tried to contain the growth of a greater Serbia. In the early years of the twentieth century wars were frequent in the Balkans.

At the Royal Geographical Society, in January 1904, the Oxford geographer, Halford Mackinder, delivered a paper that prophesied what was going to happen if territorial competition continued.[7] Eventually there would be a struggle to control the largest landmass on earth – the continent of Eurasia. If a power achieved command of that landmass it would be in a position to control the world. From a geopolitical perspective the twentieth century with the First and Second World Wars, and the Cold War, was a struggle to prevent Mackinder's prediction coming true.[8]

Although President Wilson set out some of the essentials of globalization in his Fourteen Points (1918), rapid progress towards opening the world to trade and communication has only come since the Second World War and at an increasing pace since the end of the Cold War.

Mackinder's view was present in policy-making circles until the end of the Cold War. President Carter's National Security

Adviser, Zbigniew Brzezinski, saw the Cold War as a geopolitical struggle for control over the Eurasian landmass. The Soviet Union would prevail if it could eject the West from the western and eastern fringes of Eurasia. The West would be preponderant if it contained the Soviet Union.[9]

THE DEVELOPMENT OF GLOBALIZATION

Why has it taken so long to create the mechanisms of globalization? The communication technology needed to link the world existed before the First World War,[10] but the technology was land and sea based. You needed to control a continent to build a transcontinental railroad. Telegraphy and telephones depended upon land lines and undersea cables. Ships had to come to port. In the minds of nineteenth-century statesmen to employ the technology fully you needed to control territory. Competition for territory made for belligerent international relations. There was a lack of policies to promote peaceful but competitive interaction.

After the First World War communication technology did not halt the rise of totalitarian regimes and may have aided their emergence. Today it is held that new forms of electronic communication make it difficult to seal off a population from outside sources of information. But the electronic storage and transfer of information could provide the means for state control on a scale not imagined by Stalin – although it was by George Orwell in *Nineteen Eighty-Four*.[11] Should the electronic data banks fall under the control of one force 'the empire of the world'[12] would be in sight.

Does the end of the Cold War and the opening up of so many countries to global economic forces mark the death of geopolitics? Globalization is a Western concept largely derived from Dutch and, later, Anglo-American thinking and practice. Globalization is a product of the maritime world.

The EU has free trade between member states but still utilizes many policies that close off the economic space of Europe to non-member countries. The EU is a product of the continental world. The German Chancellor of 1914 and Albert Speer could claim that the EU is the type of integrated Europe they were trying to create in the First and Second World Wars. The EU employs many of the statist policies that France, Germany and Italy favoured from 1860 to 1945. These policies, and the obstruction of free trade with non-members, cause frictions between Britain and the EU countries with land-power traditions. The United States encouraged European unification, after the Second World War, but frequently finds itself in conflict with EU policies, particularly in relation to agricultural trade. There is no unanimous view in the Western world of the policies and paths that will lead to globalization.

This book examines the interplay of geopolitical policies and the forces of globalization from the late nineteenth century to the present. Statesmen in the second half of the nineteenth century viewed the world geopolitically. Power and status depended upon the control of territory and resources. The geopolitical view was as strongly represented in the US as it was in Europe. British statesmen were interested in globalization, as the policy of free trade indicated, but British defence analysts were fearful of Europe coming under the control of one power. Chapter 1 shows how this view was powerfully set out by Halford Mackinder in 1904.

The pursuit of geopolitical policies leading to the First World War – described as a struggle for the control of resources, routeways, and productive capacity – is discussed in chapter 2. France and Britain were driven by a fear that Germany would dominate Central Europe and use that region as the base for continental control. This was exactly what Germany intended. In September 1914 the war was going well for Germany and the Chancellor drafted an outline of the peace terms he was prepared to grant the allies. The Russian empire in Eastern Europe would be broken up, there would be territorial gains at the expense of France and Belgium and a European Economic Association would be established with Germany as the hegemonic power. The EEA did not emerge from the First World War but the proposed arrangement was a forerunner of the EU, in which Germany is a senior partner rather than the hegemon.

This is followed by a discussion in chapter 3 of how geopolitically the First World War created more problems than it solved in that the peace treaties balkanized East Europe and created vulnerable new states. Several commentators immediately predicted trouble. Mackinder predicted that there would be war between Germany and Russia for control of East Europe. Isaiah Bowman, the leading US territorial specialist at Versailles, was deeply pessimistic – war would come in a few years.

Coudenhove-Kalergi was not so pessimistic for he thought the problems of Franco-German antagonism could be overcome in a European Union. Several leading French politicians including the foreign minister Briand favoured this view and pressed the idea at the League of Nations. The idea was submerged, but not obliterated, by the Depression and the rise of totalitarian regimes.

The next two chapters examine the collapse of the old world order after the First World War and show how in the Second World War Germany quickly overran Europe and set about creating a Europe that was self-sufficient and integrated economically. It is true that Hitler favoured *Blitzkrieg* economics in which raw materials, manpower, and machines were stripped out of conquered territory but technocrats like Albert Speer saw that if Germany was to win the war the manufacturing capacity of Western Europe had to be integrated with that of Germany. Many French politicians who had advocated European union before the war were favourable to Speer's ideas, including Prime Minister Laval in Vichy, France.

France and Germany had done little trade before the Second World War but by 1943 they were major trade partners and the iron and steel industry of Western Europe had been partially integrated with that of Germany. The foundations of the Coal and Steel Community (1951) and the European Economic Community (1957) were laid in the Second World War. And it was not just in Europe that new economic groupings were emerging. During the war Mexico and Canada became major trade partners with the US, foreshadowing the creation of NAFTA. In the Far East Japan established a Greater East Asia Co-Prosperity Sphere which anticipated the vast investments of Japanese *keiretsu*, on the Pacific Rim, in the postwar era.

The USSR won the war and was able to retain the closed-space, centrally planned, self-sufficient system and expand it into East Europe. The defeated powers of Germany, Japan and Italy were opened up to some of the forces of globalization and enjoyed economic expansion.

The main concern of the US in planning the postwar world was to open up markets so that expanded American manufacturing capacity would not contract when the production of war materials stopped (see chapter 6). Britain's system of imperial preference tariffs had to go, sterling had to be made convertible into dollars and Europe was to be integrated into a customs union to make European markets less complicated for US corporations exporting to, or operating in, the region. The Marshall plan helped refinance the European economy for it was recognized that there would be little trade with Europe if Europe did not recover economically.

At first the US thought that Britain would take the lead on European economic integration. However, the UK could not assume any additional financial burdens and Britain's leading trade partners before and during the war were the US and Commonwealth countries. The US could never present a consistent view of what it meant by European economic integration. Ernest Bevin and Dean Acheson understood they wanted a customs union with free trade between members and low-level tariffs for goods entering the region. Bevin had little support in the Cabinet and other US policy makers had views that differed from the Secretary of State.

The chance for British leadership passed and the US encouraged Jean Monnet to broker integration. The result was the Coal and Steel Community (1951), a plan developed without consultation with Britain. The protectionist and statist EEC (1957) followed. The Kennedy administration told Britain to apply for membership but when the UK did this in 1962 General de Gaulle vetoed the application.[13] De Gaulle was determined not to have a North Atlantic free trade area and Britain was seen as the agent that would change the tariff-protected space of the European Common Market into a free trade zone. Too late the US realized that the EEC was not a step on the way to an Atlantic community but with the Berlin Wall, the

Cuban Missile Crisis and Vietnam it was no time to argue with allies like France, Germany and Italy.

President Roosevelt thought that, with the establishment of the United Nations, there would be no need for alliances and spheres of influence at the end of the war. This view was quickly superseded by postwar geopolitical policies to contain the Soviet Union. The establishment of NATO (1949) and the rearmament of West Germany were met by the creation of the Warsaw Pact (1955) which secured the Soviet sphere of influence in East Europe. The world was divided into geopolitical power blocs and the West and the East struggled for influence in Third World countries.

The postwar era saw the triumph of geopolitics (see chapter 7). However, as George Kennan had observed in 'The Sources of Soviet Conduct', the Soviet system carried within it the seeds of its own decay. Thus chapter 8 examines the death of geopolitics along with the rapid increase in globalization. By the 1980s there was a widespread sense that centrally planned economies run by state bureaucracies could not grow at the same pace as free market systems. Living standards were rising little in the USSR and East Europe. In the Third World countries of Africa, Latin America and southeast Asia there was growing awareness that state control of economic activity led to stagnation. Rapidly, in the late 1980s and early 1990s, East Europe emerged from Soviet control, the two Germanies unified, and the Union of Soviet Socialist Republics became a Commonwealth of Independent States. Across the Third World, economies were opened up to global competitive forces and the uncomfortable reality of the free flow of capital. Not all countries, including Russia, Belarus and the Ukraine, have shown the ability to operate effectively in a global economy.

Beyond the Western world different traditions of organizing space and interacting with distant lands prevail.[14] Samuel Huntington has predicted a *Clash of Civilizations*[15] as the differing world views of the Chinese, Indic, and Islamic cultural realms are brought increasingly into contact with the Western way of organizing the globe legally, politically and economically. US foreign policy actions sometimes create unwanted responses that are vividly described by Chalmers Johnson in *Blowback*.[16]

In the nineteenth century, competitors of Britain reacted against the imperialism of free trade.[17] Already there is resentment at the emblems of American commerce that appear as the flags of globalization across the world. The imperialism of globalization will be resisted in many non-Western cultures, even if we move from an era of conflict to one of accommodation.[18] Globalization has impacts beyond economics, for it is creating a runaway world in which existing political, cultural and social relations are altered as global forces impinge on communities, families and educational systems.[19]

Imperialism, Globalization, Geopolitics

From one perspective imperialism involves globalization. Core countries reach across the world to obtain products and resources unavailable in the home territory and create trans-global linkages. But once imperial powers took possession of territory and controlled access to colonies, they partitioned earth space in ways which prevented free interchange. The European overseas empires, with the exception of the Dutch, used mercantilist policies. Settlers were usually nationals of the colonial power, trade was conducted through designated ports, the colony shipped products to the metropolitan power and received goods from that source in ships flying the national flag.

In theory the mercantilist system should break down with industrialization in the core countries of the colonial system. Industries should buy raw materials from the nearest source to cut transport costs. Imported foodstuffs should come from the cheapest producers to keep living costs, and wages, low.

Britain, the first major industrializer, began to follow the low-cost path when the repeal of the corn laws (1846) let in cheap wheat. Shortly sugar was imported more cheaply from Cuba than Barbados or Jamaica. The British adopted free trade. Tariffs were reduced and trading partners treated more equally. British colonies no longer had protected markets in the UK.

Few other countries followed a policy of free trade, partly because by the 1840s free trade with Britain was a trade between unequals.[1] Britain had more products and cheaper manufactured goods to sell than any other player. Rather than adopting free trade, countries strengthened nationalist economic policies to protect and encourage home-based industries. Countries like France continued to favour items produced in French colonies, partly because payment was in francs rather than pounds sterling. There was a deep-seated desire for self-sufficiency and a perceived need to control sources of imported foodstuffs and raw materials. Such policies can be seen as a sensible securing of long-term supplies but when imperial governments adopted practices designed to disadvantage other powers, a dangerously competitive environment was created which perpetuated itself as discrimination brought retaliation, accompanied by distrust and aggravation.

By 1890 the major players on the international game board were the land-based empires of Germany, Russia, Austria-Hungary and the Ottomans. France was a major land power, in possession of an extensive overseas empire. Britain possessed a large colonial empire supported by the Royal Navy and a fleet of merchant ships. Japan, like Britain, was an offshore island with limited resources. Japan wanted colonies and the resources they possessed. The United States had a better resource base and more room to manoeuvre than the other players. With the Louisiana Purchase (1803), the Monroe Doctrine (1823) and a belief in manifest destiny (more powerful than a policy for it was a dogma shared by all political interests) the US established a position from which it could control events in the Western hemisphere.

All the players could gain advantages from interaction and all, except Britain, avoided opening their territory up to competition. The European continental players worked to create barriers between themselves, and the US had adopted high tariffs in 1862.

Germany occupied a central location in Europe and was well placed to interact economically with surrounding countries. Several navigable rivers including the Rhine, Danube, Elbe, Weser and Oder linked German economic space with the North Sea, the Baltic and the Black Seas. The railway system was a network that served most regions of Germany efficiently and was connected to the rails of adjoining countries.

Given friendly relations with surrounding states Germany, with a central position and industrial regions in the Rhine-Ruhr, Saxony, the Saar and Silesia, together with growing technological leadership in the steel, chemical and electrical industries, was well placed to interact profitably with the rest of Europe.

Policy-makers in Germany perceived her central position as a potential weakness for the country was surrounded by major powers. Leaders stood in fear of an encircling coalition. As Henry Kissinger states:

> If Germany tried to protect itself against a coalition of all its neighbors – East and West – simultaneously, it was certain to threaten them individually, speeding up the formation of coalitions. Self-fulfilling prophecies became a part of the international system.[2]

Historically, the natural boundaries of France had formed a hexagon with sides that lay at the Alps, the Mediterranean Sea, the Pyrenees, the Atlantic, the English Channel and the Rhine.[3] The Franco-Prussian war, with the French loss of Alsace and Lorraine, had pushed France back from the Rhine. France lost iron ore and other resources in Lorraine. France lacked enough coal resources and imports were needed from Britain and Germany. With the largest agricultural sector in Europe, France had a high degree of self-sufficiency, and colonial imports, particularly from Algeria, supplied many needs.

Britain was the most globalized of the powers in 1890. The country imported foodstuffs and raw materials to feed urban workforces and supply industries with minerals and fibres. Britain exported coal and manufactured goods around the world. By value the UK imported more than it exported but more than half the merchant ships in the world were British built, owned and operated. London was the world's financial centre and a source of capital that was invested in any part of the world which offered secure conditions. In 1890 more British capital was being invested on the Rio de la Plata than in Canada or Australia.

By 1890 Britain's position as a manufacturing power was slipping. The US and Germany were outgrowing her industrially and neither country was a free trader. The influx of German goods into Britain caused alarm and from 1896 President McKinley imposed higher tariffs to protect US industries. The economic philosophy of free trade came under attack in Britain after Joseph Chamberlain's call for Tariff Reform – protectionism – in 1903.[4] Free trade survived at the time but the political foundations of protection were laid and a system of imperial preference was adopted in the Depression. Like France, Britain was feeling insecure and the insecurity stemmed from the perceived threat of Germany.[5]

By the 1890s Britain was the centre of a worldwide economic system based upon freedom of navigation, free trade, free movement of capital and the rule of law to promote economic development and protect overseas investments. No other country had as much to lose economically as Britain in a war that disrupted her trading links.

Within the borders of the multi-ethnic Russian empire were deposits of all the minerals needed to create heavy industries. The empire was technologically backward and capital, for major projects, was scarce. Strategically the country was isolated. Baltic ports like St Petersburg iced up and shut down in winter. The ports on the Arctic coast were remote and only open for a few months of the year, although in the west, Murmansk, on the Barents Sea, was close enough to the unfrozen waters of the north Atlantic to remain open all year. Some Black Sea ports, which connected the empire to the Mediterranean, were ice free. The Pacific ports were distant until the completion of a trans-Siberia railway early in the twentieth century. Even so, the journey from Moscow to Vladivostok took weeks.

The Russian empire needed the technology and investment skills available in Western Europe if it was to grow economically but, with low living standards, the empire was nearly self-sufficient. The empire's connections with the outside world were not essential as they were in the case of Britain.

All the lesser players in Europe including Italy, Belgium, the Netherlands and Luxembourg illustrated the need for economic cooperation rather than conflict. Italy lacked many raw materials but international trade could correct that. Luxembourg, with plentiful iron ore, needed Germany's coal and did join a customs union with Germany. Belgium's metallurgical industries had markets and suppliers in the Ruhr and northern France. Antwerp was a port that served northern France and parts of Germany as well as Belgium. The Netherlands, with colonies in the Caribbean and southeast Asia, needed peace to prosper for much economic activity depended on the connections of Rotterdam and Amsterdam with trade along the Rhine. Belgium and the Netherlands were neutrals but even if neutrality was respected the disruption of war would reduce cross-border trade with France and Germany and diminish economic opportunities.

In the 1890s most activities were seen in national terms and league tables were constructed of who made the most steel and dug the most coal, activities perceived to be at the base of powerful industries that could sustain a country in war. The concept of opening borders to promote competition and efficiency was against ruling opinion which saw the need for tariffs to protect home industries from competition.

By the 1890s it was obvious that the United States had the area, population, resources and market to outrank any other country economically. In his farewell address George Washington had warned against foreign entanglements and there was little need for them given the available territory in North America. The Louisiana Purchase (1803) more than doubled the size of the country and brought the Mississippi–Missouri river system under US control. The purchase provided land to settle future farmers and existing ports like New Orleans, Baton Rouge and St Louis were brought into the US to serve the interior. In 1817 the Spanish were dispossessed of their territory in Florida. Texas, in independent Mexico, was settled by Americans in the 1820s. Shortly they rebelled, formed the Republic of Texas (1836), and then joined the US in 1845. A war with Mexico (1846–8) brought in territory in California, New Mexico and Arizona, via the treaty of Guadalupe Hidalgo in 1848. The Gadsden purchase (1853) largely completed land acquisitions on the southern border. In the north the boundary with Canada was adjusted in both the East and the West after the US threatened to use force. By the 1850s there was widespread talk of an empire in the Caribbean.[6]

The war between the states (1862–6) concentrated attention on internal issues and after the war the US grew rapidly as a major agricultural exporter, partially as a result of settling immigrants from Europe on federal lands in the Midwest, the Great Plains, the Rockies and the Pacific West. Much of the land had been designated as Indian territory but the rights of native peoples were ignored as the economic imperative gained control, symbolized by the opening of the transcontinental railroad in 1869. The Indians resisted dispossession and won victories as at the Little Big Horn over Custer's force in 1876. But bands of armed horsemen could not compete with a modern state and Indians were persuaded by events, like the Wounded Knee massacre, to live inconspicuously on reservations. The industrial killing of the buffalo, for their hides, contributed to the collapse of traditional lifestyles.

The US manufacturing sector grew rapidly as the new lands were settled. Expanding demand for steel, railroads, agricultural machinery, building materials and consumer goods provided markets for industries. By 1896 the McKinley tariffs were giving additional protection to American industry from European imports, although in many activities, including railroad equipment and agricultural machinery, American industries were already dominant in the home market, making products suited to the environments of North America.

The US possessed the resources of farmland, coal, iron ore, timber and non-ferrous metals to create self-sufficiency. The US had a resource advantage over Europe in the possession of oilfields which provided cheap fuel for heating, trucks and automobiles.

In the nineteenth century the US employed geopolitical policies long before the term *geopolitics* came into use. The Louisiana Purchase provided living space; the Monroe Doctrine (1823) established a sphere of influence; the insistence that the states should not impede interstate commerce with tariffs created a customs union. These developments were noted by European observers. Friedrich List (1789–1846) visited the US before publishing his book *Zollvereins – The National System of Political Economy*. Ratzel[7] travelled widely in America and Mexico prior to his academic career in which he developed the concept of *Lebensraum* – living space.

Opinion in the US was quick to sense closure as the great frontier reached the West Coast and an heroic age came to an end. The Wisconsin historian Frederick Jackson Turner[8] delivered a paper on the closing of the American frontier at Chicago in 1893 in which he argued that the settling of the frontier had been a process in which America constantly renewed itself and that era was coming to an end. The paper is an example of closed-space thinking[9] and it appeared at just the time when technological developments were, in fact, opening up new possibilities for economic growth – possibilities that were not dependent upon more territory on which to settle more farmers.

Many thought that the US, having attained manifest destiny, with the country spread from sea to shining sea, should look outwards and take a larger role in world affairs. Foremost among writers promoting an imperial future for America was Admiral Alfred Thayer Mahan in a book entitled *The Influence of Seapower Upon History, 1660–1783*, published in 1890.[10]

For the most part *The Influence of Seapower* is a conventional history of naval warfare to the end of the American Revolution. It is difficult to believe that the book became a bestseller on the basis of stories of wooden sailing ships armed with canons and cutlasses but chapter 1 carried a powerful message for US policy-makers. The opening of the Panama Canal would transform the Caribbean from a terminus into a major sea route, linking the Pacific and Atlantic Oceans.

> Along this path a great commerce will travel, bringing the interests of the other great nations, the European nations, close along our shores … With this it will not be so easy as heretofore to stand aloof from international complications.[11]

The US would need a navy and bases in the Caribbean to protect the Gulf Coast. Further, as America traded around the world, it would need distant bases and capital ships capable of projecting power.[12] The US, lying between two old worlds and two great oceans, was destined by geography to play a leading role in world affairs.

Teddy Roosevelt reviewed *The Influence of Seapower* and endorsed the naval policy Mahan was suggesting.[13] Mahan was widely read in US political circles but it will never be possible to establish whether or not the book had a direct influence on policy.

Mahan's opinions reflected ideas that were already in circulation. Roosevelt, the president who launched the Great White Fleet around the world in 1908, already believed the US needed a navy of capital ships at the time *Influence* appeared.[14] New views were in the air and Mahan caught the changing tide of opinion at the right moment. Events followed rapidly.

In 1896 Hawaii was annexed to provide a naval base in the Pacific and to forestall any intentions the Japanese had towards the island group. In 1898, after a short war with Spain, the US acquired the Philippines, Guam, Puerto Rico and Caribbean bases, including Guantánamo Bay in Cuba. Early in the new century Britain reduced her naval presence in the Caribbean. In 1903 Panama broke away from Colombia and entered into an agreement whereby the US would take over the failed French diggings and complete, at US government expense, a canal linking the Caribbean and the Pacific. The canal was to be large enough to allow US warships to move quickly between the Atlantic and the Pacific.

In 1900 Mahan published *The Problem of Asia and its Effects upon International Policies*.[15] The volume originated as magazine articles patched together to make a book that is repetitive and never easy to read. However, Mahan does comment on many of the issues which have been prominent in international affairs through to the present. Mahan thought that the major powers were in a phase of expansion and were exercising 'a right to grow'.[16] Growth would be achieved by a 'natural selection'[17] in which the strong would expand at the expense of the weak, not necessarily by war. Indigenous peoples on the periphery did not have 'natural rights', and resources in the territory they occupied had to be developed for the general good using compulsion if necessary.[18] This type of social Darwinism was common at the turn of the century, and Sharp recounts the story of Lord Salisbury, at the Foreign Office, presiding over the woes of dead and dying states, with living nations encroaching on the territory of the dying.[19]

When he looked at the map Mahan saw that the Russian empire occupied a vast area in the interior of Asia remote from the sea. This was an economic disadvantage which Mahan proposed to remedy by giving the empire better access to the coast of

China.[20] Other powers should also have easier entry into China to promote economic development.[21]

Mahan saw a special relationship between Britain and the US[22] and thought the North Atlantic was the centre of the 'old community of European civilization upon which, from our point of view, the welfare of humanity rests'.[23]

'France lay outside the North Atlantic community as indicated by her alliance with Russia.'[24] Japan had modernized and could, along with Germany, provide restraint on the flanks of the Russian empire.

Mahan thought the world was entering a phase of boundary readjustments and the US would not be able to stand aside if there was going to be a major change in the European balance of power.[25] The US was drawn into the First World War to prevent the central powers from dominating Europe. The war revealed the diminished role of sea power as the Baltic and Black Seas were closed off to the navies of the Western allies.

The decline of sea power had already been predicted by the British geographer, Halford Mackinder. On the night of Monday, 25 January 1904, Mackinder delivered a lecture to the Royal Geographical Society entitled 'The Geographical Pivot of History'. Mackinder started in a novel way, telling the audience that the Columbian epoch, the age of sea power, was coming to an end. Land power was about to reassert itself; sea power, the basis of Britain's position as a great power, was declining.[26]

Mackinder argued that in the closed heartland of Eurasia there was a pivotal region that lay beyond the reach of sea power. The pivot lay in the drainage basins of the Ob, Yenisey and Lena, which fell into the Arctic, and the Volga and Oxus rivers which fed the Caspian and Aral Seas (illus. 1). When the railways were built this vast interior region would produce increased quantities of wheat, cotton, fuels, and metals while remaining apart from oceanic commerce.[27] Under Stalin's five-year plans the Volga, the Urals, Siberia and Central Asia, which lie in the pivot, were developed.[28] Had the Soviet economy not been spread eastward, but remained concentrated in European Russia instead, it is likely the USSR would have lost the Second World War.

At the time Mackinder spoke the pivot region was not developed but, like Mahan, Mackinder thought power balances would shift. He considered the contenders for control of the pivot. The Chinese, organized by the Japanese, were a possible candidate and if China got control it would add oceanic frontage to the resources of the pivot region, an advantage that 'the Russian tenant' of the region did not possess.[29] But Mackinder feared most an alliance of Germany and Russia. And the major contenders for control of Eurasia in the twentieth century were Germany and the Russian empire/Soviet Union. The alliance the USSR and Germany did make (1939–41) was short-lived but during it Germany received large quantities of raw materials to sustain itself as it overran Western Europe and evaded the British blockade.

There have been many criticisms of Mackinder's thesis[30] but some of the most interesting points were made by L. S. Amery in the discussion at the RGS that immediately followed the paper. A few weeks before Mackinder spoke the Wright brothers had flown at Kittyhawk on the Atlantic coast of North Carolina. Amery pointed out that air power might make the land power vs. sea power debate obsolete. Amery suggested, perhaps thinking that not enough attention had been paid to the US, that in the future 'the people who have the industrial power and the power of invention and of science will be able to defeat all others'.[31] It would not matter if they were on an island or in the centre of a continent. Amery could comment incisively because he understood the pivot concept and utilized aspects of it when he was a policy-maker in the First and Second World Wars. Both Mackinder and Amery made the point that forces reverberated around the globe and, as Amery put it, there was a tendency to look at policy-making as if the world was cut up into watertight compartments whereas any action in one part of the world affected international relations in all parts of the globe.[32]

As the leading German geographer of his day, Friedrich Ratzel (1844–1904) had ideas on how Germany was to acquire enough territory to become a world power – *Weltmacht*. As a student at Heidelberg, Ratzel studied geology and zoology and was influenced by Darwinian ideas. After active service in the Franco-Prussian war (1870–71) Ratzel became a foreign correspondent, travelling in the US and Mexico between 1873 and 1875 before teaching at Munich and Leipzig.[33]

As a geographer Ratzel was interested in the impact of environmental influences upon human activity. His book *Anthropogeographie* was widely read and his environmentally deterministic approach was brought to the US by Ellen Churchill Semple. Semple studied with Ratzel in Germany and published *The Influences of Geographic Environment on the Basis of Ratzel's System of Anthropogeography* (1911) which was widely read by geographers and historians in the US.

Ratzel's political geography concept of *Lebensraum* (living space) was based upon natural history and Darwinian thinking. Organisms adapted to the space they occupied. If they were successful they colonized surrounding territory and increased their *Lebensraum*. Successful organisms grew at the expense of weaker organisms.[34] Ratzel applied this thinking to the life of states:

> The growth of states proceeds through the annexation of small territories ... while at the same time the attachment of the people to the soil becomes ever closer ...[35]

It followed from this that states had a right to grow. Ratzel was blunt:

> The territory of a state is no definite area fixed for all time – for a state is a living organism and therefore cannot be contained within rigid limits – being dependent for its form and greatness on its inhabitants, in whose movements, outwardly exhibited especially in territorial growth or contraction, it participates.[36]

The world had arrived at a dangerous point by the time statements such as these were finding their way into academic journals and policy-making circles. Already there was an awareness of the increasing size of states and the acceptance of Darwinian notions of survival of the fittest in international affairs. Influential writers like Mahan and Ratzel suggested that strong states had the right to expansion. This rendered the existing system of states obsolete and required a reordering of territory. It is easy to suggest that the ideas of Mahan and Ratzel had limited circulation, but these writers were putting a quasi-academic gloss on notions that were widely discussed popularly and in policy-making circles.

It used to be argued that Ratzel was writing as an academic[37] but Bassin has shown that he was heavily involved in German imperial political issues and an advocate of German overseas expansion and a large German fleet.[38] One commentator has concluded that, whatever Ratzel's intentions, he 'created a means of legitimating an imperialist ideology from science'.[39]

Had Ratzel's work remained solely in the academic arena it would now be regarded as another quaint example of Darwinian social science seeking laws of human behaviour in analogies from biology. Ratzel's ideas were taken up by the politically active Swedish social scientist, Rudolf Kjellén, and it was Kjellén, in 1899, who coined the term *Geopolitik*. Kjellén's 1905 book *Stormakterna* (*The Great Powers*) argued for the development of superstates and an enlarged Germany. *Stormakterna* was published in Sweden but made little impact. There were, however, 22 German editions of the book, the last published in 1930, edited by Karl Haushofer, the leading geopolitician in Nazi Germany.[40]

In 1898 France and Britain gave themselves a fright at Fashoda[41] on the upper White Nile. Imperial imaginations had created a Cape-to-Cairo route for Britain and a West Africa-to-the-Red-Sea route for France. The perceived routeways intersected on the White Nile when a French expedition, coming from the west, attempted to claim Fashoda as a Nile port. The claim was resisted by Britain. Conflict approached. The folly of risking war over imagined routeways, in barren territory, at the heart of an inaccessible continent, was realized. Britain and France decided to improve relations; the result was the *Entente Cordiale* (1904).

In the afterglow of the signing of the *Entente*, King Edward VII, who had played a central role in improving relations with France, asked if the same could be done with Germany.

At the Foreign Office, a career civil servant, Eyre Crowe (1864–1925), prepared a paper entitled 'Memorandum on the Present State of British Relations with France and Germany'. The long memorandum, dated 1 January 1907, was printed and widely read in government circles. The document was pessimistic and forecast German expansion and a determination to become a world power holding more colonies.

Eyre Crowe had a good knowledge of Germany – he had been born in Leipzig to a German mother and was educated in various gymnasia as his British consul father took up posts in Düsseldorf and Berlin. In 1903 Eyre Crowe married a well-connected German widow and made frequent visits to Germany.

According to Crowe, the idea of a large colonial empire had taken hold of the German imagination. The Emperor, statesmen, journalists, geographers, economists, commercial interests and the mass of educated and uneducated opinion declared with one voice:

> We *must* have real Colonies, where German emigrants can settle and spread the national ideals of the Fatherland, and we *must* have a fleet and coaling stations to keep together the Colonies which we are bound to acquire. To the question, 'Why *must*?' the ready answer is: 'A healthy and powerful State like Germany, with its 60,000,000 inhabitants, must expand, it cannot stand still, it must have territories to which its overflowing population can emigrate without giving up its nationality.' When it is objected that the world is now actually parcelled out among independent States, and that territory for colonization cannot be had except by taking it from the rightful possessor, the reply again is: 'We cannot enter into such considerations. Necessity has no law. The world belongs to the strong. A vigorous nation cannot allow its growth to be hampered by blind adherence to the *status quo*. We have no designs on other people's possessions, but where States are too feeble to put their territory to the best possible use, it is the manifest destiny of those who can and will do so to take their places ...[42]

Given that Germany was building a fleet of Dreadnought battleships and enlarged the Kiel canal to allow the fleet to move rapidly from the Baltic to the North Sea the material on German expansion was worrying.

Eyre Crowe did not advocate a British effort to accommodate Germany. In fact he thought one-sided bargains with Germany should be avoided and Britain should uphold her interests throughout the world. A policy of strength was the only way to win the respect of the German nation.

There are parallels between Eyre Crowe's long memorandum and George Kennan's long telegram of 1946. Both advocate a firm stance to contain expansion and stress the need to let the expansionist power know that force will be used. That was the way to deter aggression.

Before the outbreak of war in 1914 Eyre Crowe advised that Britain should tell Germany, unequivocally, that if Germany attacked France, Britain would enter the war. The warning was never issued. Britain did not ally with France until war started in August 1914 (illus. 2).

In spite of great power competition globalization was developing before the First World War. World trade was expanding rapidly, gold provided a global currency and a mechanism for settling international debts. The cross-border movement of capital for investment purposes was common. The middle and professional classes travelled internationally and ideas flowed readily from one country to another. Britain and the US adopted many German education models. German science was particularly important in the chemical and textile industries and patent laws safeguarded the work of those making new discoveries. Trade between Britain and Germany was increasing rapidly with the balance in favour of Germany – only the US did more trade with Britain than Germany. Many believed that there was nothing concrete for Germany and Britain to fight

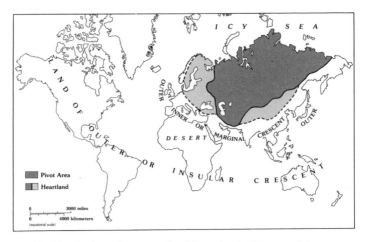

1 Halford Mackinder – The geographical 'Pivot Area' of history and the 'Heartland', from *Geographical Journal* (April 1904) and *Democratic Ideals and Reality* (1919).

2 The boundaries of European states on the eve of the First World War.

over.[43] But Britain feared a future German dominance in Eurasia. Germany thought Britain was an obstacle to her great power status.

The war damaged all the European players. Germany lost territory in Europe and all her overseas possessions. France lost over a million men in a war that devastated the northern part of the country. The Russian empire collapsed as did the empire of Austria-Hungary. Britain's central role in world trade was damaged. London never regained its dominance as the world's leading financial centre and sterling's position as the dominant currency of world trade was weakened.

Worst of all, the war did not settle any of the geopolitical issues that had caused the conflict. Postwar Europe was full of the small, weak states that the geopoliticians thought to be vulnerable. The empire of Austria-Hungary, which had shared economic space, a customs union and a common currency, was destroyed, although out of the wreckage came a number of important economists and political thinkers who were active in developing the theory of international, cooperative economic organizations (chapter 4). Defeated Germany produced a new breed of destructive geopoliticians. Hardly had the new states emerged from the defunct empire of Austria-Hungary than the illegitimate heirs of Ratzel targeted them for destruction, long before the Nazi party came to power.[44] The path to the Second World War was to lead straight through the territory of the new states created in the wake of the First World War.

The Geopolitics of the First World War, 1914–19

The First World War was not an ideological nor a dynastic war. It was a war fought with the aim of controlling territory, resources, industrial regions and routeways.[1] The empires of Germany, Russia, Austria-Hungary and Japan all wanted to enlarge themselves. France and Italy had the same aim. Britain, and to some degree the US, were adopting globalization policies before the First World War but the UK, and then the US, were pulled into the war by a fear that the central powers would control so much of mainland Europe that they would pose a threat to trade and the maritime, Atlantic world. You cannot practise globalization if other powers aim to exclude you from major world regions like Europe.

The war aims of France in 1914 included reclaiming Alsace-Lorraine, acquiring the coal resources of the Saar and the creation of a Rhineland state that would weaken Germany and act as a buffer between France and Germany.[2]

The Russian war aims included long-standing territorial aims: control of the straits leading from the Black Sea into the Mediterranean, more influence in Eastern Europe (Russia entered the war to support Serbia against Austria) and more ports on the Baltic.[3] The Gulf of Finland freezes in the winter leaving St Petersburg landlocked for several months. The Baltic ice problem lessens to the west and to the south so that Riga, in Russian-controlled Latvia, had a longer ice-free period than St Petersburg. The German ports of Memel and Königsberg (Klaipèda and Kalliningrad today) usually did not freeze up and Russia wanted them, along with their hinterlands, for the great land power was short of ports.

British war aims were complex. The UK, with prewar policies

of free trade, free movement of capital and freedom of navigation, had a commitment to globalization. Britain also had an
empire constructed on geostrategic principles. Britain would be
forced to pursue geopolitical policies if the central powers disturbed territorial balances. On the surface Britain entered the
war to protect Belgian neutrality, which the UK had guaranteed
in the treaty of London (1839). Britain's interest went much further than Belgium.[4] Sir Edward Grey, the foreign secretary at
the start of the war, believed that if Germany took Belgium then
other small countries, like the Netherlands and Denmark, would
come under German control. Grey thought it impossible for
Britain to stand aloof if the German fleet attacked the French
Channel ports and disrupted trade with Britain. Above all if
Britain let Western Europe fall 'under the domination of a single
power' then she would be powerless to alter the result.[5] Germany
would be dominant in Europe. The fear of allowing Europe to
fall under the control of one power is embedded in Western
defence policy during the twentieth century and was well developed in the writings of A. T. Mahan and H. J. Mackinder. And
Grey, having been, along with Mackinder, a member of the Co-
Efficients dining club, where defence issues were discussed, was
aware of Mackinder's views.[6]

Grey, to prevent *any* power becoming dominant in Europe,
strove during the war to maintain power balances. Grey did not
want Germany and Austria-Hungary destroyed. Nor did he
want Russia and France to become too powerful. Grey worked
to keep 'Russia out of Prague, Vienna, Budapest, Belgrade,
Bucharest and Sofia', and 'France out of Cologne, Mainz and
Koblenz'.[7]

Britain had interests to protect beyond Europe. In the
Middle East, the Ottoman empire had allied itself with the central powers. This was a threat given that Germany had plans to
build a railway from Berlin to Baghdad which would give access
to the Persian Gulf and the Indian Ocean. Geostrategically
Britain had to protect the Suez Canal, Gulf oil interests and the
Indian empire. Making allies of tribes in Arabia might destabilize the Ottoman empire and eventually provide additional
client states to add to the colonies and protectorates at places
like Aden, Oman, Bahrein, Kuwait and Cyprus that under-

pinned the British position in the Middle East. Here was an uncomfortable principle of policy driven by geostrategy – it always seemed necessary to take on additional positions to protect existing interests.

Japan had extensive war aims in the Far East. In 1902 Britain and Japan signed an alliance that required the countries to aid each other if either was attacked by *two* states. Japan rapidly entered the First World War to protect British shipping against German raiders in the Far East and to grab German possessions at Shantung in China and the German Pacific colonies north of the Equator – the Caroline, Mariana and Marshall Islands. The Shantung peninsula was not Japan's only ambition in relation to China. In 1915 China was presented with 21 demands which would have placed many constraints on Chinese policy-making and put the country within Japan's sphere of influence. The demands were rejected by China but later the US agreed to acknowledge Japan's special position in relation to China in the Lansing-Ishii Agreement (2 November 1917). Japan did well out of the First World War, becoming a member of the Council of the League of Nations. China entered the war on 4 August 1917 and received few rewards. Shantung remained with Japan.[8]

Britain, France and Russia made territorial promises to induce other countries to join the war on their side. Under the secret treaty of London (26 April 1915), Italy joined the war against Austria, on 23 May 1915, in return for promises of Alpine territory, Trieste and Dalmatia, largely at Austrian expense and for the Turkish province of Adalia. Italy did not declare war on Germany until August 1916 and suffered defeats against the armies of Austria. As in the Second World War when Italy was on the side of Germany, she entered the war for territorial gain and proved a liability to her allies.

In August 1916 Romania was promised Hungarian territory by the allies and entered the war against the central powers. Most of Romania was soon overrun by the armies of the central powers.

When all the contestants had entered the war, two were recognized as the most powerful – Germany and the United States, countries sharing geopolitical histories with parallels. By colonization, warfare, purchase, negotiation, threat and displacement the US had assumed its manifest destiny and spread across the resource-rich continent of North America. Now the US wanted to look outward and interact with the wider world. It was beginning to adopt globalization policies.

Germany, like the US, had fought wars of unification in the 1860s but was still attempting to consolidate control of a large resource base in Central Europe. Like the US Germany wanted to project outward into global affairs, but on the basis of Ratzelian, geopolitical policies of territorial control. In trying to control *Mitteleuropa* Germany alarmed its neighbours and the globalizing powers – Britain and the US – and drew them into the war to protect their interests. 'Look at the map of Europe now!' exclaimed President Wilson in November 1917:

> Germany has absolute control of Austria-Hungary, practical control of the Baltic States, control of Turkey, control of Asia minor. I saw a map in which the whole thing was printed in … black … and the black stretched all the way from Hamburg to Baghdad – the bulk of German power inserted into the heart of the world … [9]

Germany's war went well, at first. In the West German forces occupied Luxembourg, industrial Belgium and northeastern France. Paris came under threat and German leaders hoped that France would sue for peace. In a memorandum dated 9 September 1914 the German chancellor, Bethmann Hollweg, set out his ideas for Germany's demands in peace negotiations. In a negotiated peace not all of the chancellor's aims would have been achieved and the memo was made obsolete by events. But the memo reveals the ideas that were in circulation, in 1914, in German policy-making circles.[10]

The memo contains extensive territorial demands at the expense of France and Belgium. Luxembourg would become a German state. In addition, the Belgian coast along with Dunkirk, Calais and Boulogne were to be placed under German military control. In modern geostrategic terms Germany was to demand a half share of one of the European 'choke points' – the straits of Dover.

The greatest part of the memo dealt with the creation of a

European Economic Association, dominated by Germany. Within the EEA tariffs would be structured so that German products would enjoy access to European economic space and not be subject to discriminatory tariffs when, for example, they entered France. The initial members of EEA were to be France, Belgium, Holland, Denmark, Austria-Hungary and Poland. Italy, Sweden and Norway were listed as possible members. The economic objective was to secure, in the chancellor's words, 'Germany's economic dominance over *Mitteleuropa*'.[11]

From this basic model for a European Economic Community, Britain was to be specifically excluded. Britain's contribution to a negotiated peace, in 1914, was to provide African colonies so that Germany might create a continuous Central African colonial empire which would also contain former French colonies and the Belgian Congo, with the Katanga copper mines.

The chancellor's September 1914 memorandum does not give detailed plans for Eastern Europe but the intention was to break Russia's domination over the non-Russian peoples, which was done by Germany in 1918 at the treaty of Brest-Litovsk. In general the Europe that would have been created by German peace plans is set out in illustration 3.

The official German documents detailing war aims were not opened until decades later but the general ideas were widely understood in policy-making circles and broadly described in Naumann's *Mitteleuropa* (1915). At the start of the war, in Naumann's view, there were three superstates controlling large segments of earth space – the United States, the British empire and the Russian empire. To join the superstates, Germany had to become dominant in *Mitteleuropa*. The first step would be the economic union of Germany with Austria-Hungary followed by the incorporation of the economies of West and East Europe.[12]

The plan seemed rational to Naumann but it was perceived as a threat elsewhere. As W. A. S. Hewins, an authority on *Zollvereins* (customs unions), warned the House of Commons on 10 January 1916, Germany was creating an economic bloc in Europe integrated by common tariffs.[13] Many in Britain, France and later the US feared that if they accepted a German-dominated

3 A Europe dominated by Germany.

Mitteleuropa they would help lay the foundation for subsequent phases of German expansion.

A major German aim, in the First World War, was the establishment of a European Economic Association (EEA) that shared many characteristics with the EEC founded after the Second World War. Politically EEA was impossible, for Germany wanted to take territory from other members and exercise hegemonic power in the EEA. However, Bethmann Hollweg had set out in the EEA idea a model that was used to bind Germany into Europe after the Second World War. It has been argued that if Britain had stayed out of the First World War, and Germany had created the EEA, it would have been possible to reach trade agreements, in the same way that the US came to trade understandings with the EEC. If an EEA had been created in 1914, the destruction of the European economy would have been avoided and, provided the UK and the US agreed trade terms with the EEA, world trade would have grown rapidly. There are problems with this scenario. Germany saw the EEA as a mechanism for enlarging German trade at the expense of Britain, and Germany saw control of *Mitteleuropa* as a base for projecting power onto the world stage to obtain *Grossraum* and colonies. Many in Britain feared that Germany would build the fleet to back the policy. The Anglo-German antagonisms had to be resolved before positive policies could emerge.[14]

Ferguson describes how difficult it would have been to do this once the war started. German policy-making came increasingly under military control and was further removed from the concession-making needed to negotiate a peace.[15] But it is difficult to disagree with Ferguson's view that there had been sustained economic growth between 1896 and 1914, with price stability, growing world trade, and increasing capital flows. The First World War brought to an end a sustained period of economic globalization. As we shall see in the next chapter it was to take decades to recreate that situation.[16]

President Wilson thought he could save the world economy with open diplomacy and free trade. Some US policy aims were set out in *The Inquiry Memorandum* of 4 January 1918 which contains 'A suggested statement of Peace Terms'.[17] The terms are dominated by territorial issues. President Wilson had *The Inquiry Memorandum* at hand when he wrote the Fourteen Points speech delivered to a joint session of Congress on 8 January 1918.[18] However, before he went to the territorial issues the president set out, in the first five points, the general principles he wanted to use in the creation of a postwar, new world order.

I. There would be 'Open covenants of peace' and no secret diplomacy.

II. 'Absolute freedom of navigation upon the seas, outside territorial waters ... in peace and in war.'

III. 'The removal ... of all economic trade barriers, and the establishment of an equality of trade conditions among all nations consenting to the peace: and associating themselves for its maintenance.'

IV. Reduction of armaments.

V. 'Impartial adjustment of colonial claims' taking into account 'the interests of the populations concerned'.

Only after setting out a framework for improved global interaction did Wilson turn to territorial questions. The term *self-determination* did not appear in the Fourteen Points speech! In the points dealing with territorial issues President Wilson was primarily concerned with restoring the *status quo ante bellum*. The only proposal to create a new state concerned Poland, and Germany had declared an independent Poland in 1916.

A reading of Wilson's territorial points does not, necessarily, provide a basis for a Europe containing new nation states. Wilson wanted Germany out of Russia, France and Belgium (no mention of Luxembourg). Alsace-Lorraine was to be returned to France. The central powers would evacuate Serbia, Montenegro and Romania. The Italy–Austria boundary would be adjusted on the basis of nationality (good news for the German speakers in the Italian Dolomites). National groups within Austria-Hungary and the Ottoman empire were to be given an opportunity for autonomous development. In the case of Austria-Hungary this could have led to a federal framework. Austria and Hungary already had separate parliaments and the model could have been extended, at least, to Prague and Bratislava.

President Wilson concluded the points by suggesting a general association of nations to guarantee independence and national integrity. The idea for a League of Nations had been widely discussed before the outbreak of war.[19] Wilson was to give shape to the organization, and insights into his global viewpoint, when he drafted the outline for the covenants of the League later in 1918.

In the Fourteen Points speech, Wilson made a rudimentary statement of the principles of globalization. The speech was intended as the basis of a negotiated peace and the creation of a more open world with fewer barriers to trade. By 1918 the US possessed the most powerful economy in the world and freer trade would favour her interests, just as it does today.

The Fourteen Points did not become the basis of peace negotiations and President Wilson gave subsequent speeches, in the spring and summer of 1918, in which he became increasingly critical of the central powers. In the four supplementary points speech of 4 July 1918, Wilson wanted the destruction of the arbitrary powers that could disturb the peace of the world.[20]

By September the empire of Austria-Hungary was falling into ethnic pieces, the US had recognized Czechoslovakia,[21] and the Ottomans, with the Arabian provinces in rebellion, were about to sue for peace. The old order was crumbling. The statesmen were losing control. Nationalists were rampant.

The nationality principle had established a momentum of its own, before Wilson's speeches of 1918. Early in the war Britain and France began to exploit the ethnic make-up of the German empire, Austria-Hungary and the Ottoman empire. By the spring of 1915 British ministers, and their advisors, were discussing new boundaries based upon national groups, or ethnographical principles.[22] Emigré politicians from Poland, Bohemia and Serbia were listened to in London, Paris and many American cities with ethnic communities derived from Europe.

The idea of redrawing the boundaries of Central and Eastern Europe was given intellectual force by academics such as the historian R. W. Seton-Watson (1879–1951), who established himself as an authority on Austria-Hungary and the Balkans before the war started. Seton-Watson wanted Germany to give up territories inhabited by non-German populations. He wanted to see the restoration of Polish and Bohemian independence and the completion of Italian, Romanian, Yugoslav and Greek unification. Seton-Watson collected around him an influential group of scholars in London, including the future president of Czechoslovakia, T. G. Masaryk, who taught at Kings College. The group published a journal, *The New Europe*, from 1916 to 1920 as an outlet for ideas on the form of new states.[23] The group regarded the large land empires as bad for they represented a concentration of power in a few hands in a few capital cities. The rise of centralized empires had obscured the regional and provincial diversity of Europe and the power of communities to control their own affairs. Big states were bad for democracy. The argument could be made in the context of Europe in 1918 but it meant that the nationality principle, the concept of self-determination, could not be applied to Germany, if you wished to downsize that country. If the *Volksdeutsche* in Denmark, Poland, the Sudetenland, Austria, Hungary, northern Italy, Alsace, Lithuania and Latvia were given self-determination then Germany might expand in size.

The principle of self-determination could not be applied to Germany because Germany could lose the war and still achieve territorial expansion. Self-determination was not a principle that could be consistently applied.[24]

Few saw the disadvantages of creating new states that might erect barriers to the free movement of goods and capital. Robert Lansing, the US Secretary of State for Foreign Affairs (1915–30), thought that self-determination would bring instability and, because national groups did not occupy easily delimited territory, it would be difficult to create new states containing one national group.[25] Lansing, a northerner, doubted there was a principle of self-determination but, if it existed, why hadn't the American south been allowed to exercise the principle in 1861, when the southern states wished to secede from the Union? A civil war had been fought to preserve the Union and the extensive economic space that manifest destiny had created. The industrializing north needed the markets and raw materials of the south.

The First World War did not end with a worldwide negotiated peace. The fighting went on until the powers became exhausted, one by one. Russia sued for peace with Germany at the end of 1917 and signed the treaty of Brest-Litovsk on 3 March 1918. Romania made a peace with the central powers in January 1918. Bulgaria capitulated to the allies on 30 September 1918. Turkey did the same on 31 October, and Austria-Hungary followed on 3 November 1918. In the West, Britain and France, reinforced by US entry into the war (April 1917), were able to withstand the powerful German offensives in the spring of 1918. By September, the German military knew that their manpower resources were reaching exhaustion. Defeat was inevitable. The senior officers resigned. A civilian government was given the task of treating for peace. The Kaiser abdicated on 9 November and went to the Netherlands where he was given asylum. Germany signed an armistice on 11 November which made it impossible, in the short run, to restart the war. German troops withdrew from allied territories, armaments were handed over, the German Rhineland was occupied by allied troops.

In the armistice there was no sign of Wilson's ideas on globalization and little of them in the peace treaties that formally concluded the war. The treaties were drawn up on a geopolitical basis. Concepts of globalization and improved interaction between states were mostly absent. Germany understood the geopolitics of the peace and was to work, almost without interruption, to rearm, regain lost territory, reassert influence in *Mitteleuropa* and, under Hitler, establish hegemony over Europe.

THREE

Who Rules East Europe Commands the Heartland

The map of mainland Europe, in the spring of 1914, had been dominated by extensive empires. Only in the Balkans was a region divided into many relatively small states. By 1922 Eastern Europe and the Middle East had been Balkanized (illus. 4–6).

The allied powers never had a coherent vision of the form of postwar Europe. Britain, France and the US all had different views. Further, their former ally, the Russian empire, had collapsed, left the war early, and now was a Bolshevik state, cutting itself off from the world. The Russian collapse had facilitated the emergence of new states with Baltic shores but Bolshevism was feared. Very quickly the idea emerged of Germany as a bulwark against the Bolsheviks. Early in 1919, L. S. Amery suggested that if the West wanted to prevent Bolshevism coming to the Rhine,

> we had better go to the Germans ... with terms involving no humiliating loss of territory, a reasonable indemnity, and no disarmament but ... a request to the Germans to cooperate with us in defending the line of the Eastern Polish Frontier ... [1]

The idea of getting Germany in the Western camp to protect against Bolshevism became established in the British view, Lloyd George in the Fontainebleau memorandum (25 March 1919) feared that Germany would

> throw in her lot with Bolshevism and place her resources, her brains, her vast organizing power at the disposal of the revolutionary fanatics whose dream it is to conquer the world for Bolshevism.[2]

4 Mackinder's New Europe, *c.* 1919.

Prime Minister Lloyd George and Leo Amery indicated the need to bind Germany into Europe or run the risk that she would ally with the Soviet Union and realize Mackinder's fear that should Germany and Russia form an alliance the empire of the world would be in sight.

Germany was dealt with harshly at Versailles but not broken up. From a geopolitical perspective the postwar world favoured German expansion in Europe. In the Danube Valley Germany was not faced by the empire of Austria-Hungary but by a gaggle of smaller states. In Eastern Europe, Germany did not have a boundary with the Russian empire or the Soviet Union but a boundary with Poland, beyond which lay the weak Baltic states of Lithuania, Latvia and Estonia. They, with Finland, were friendly to Germany for their independence had resulted from

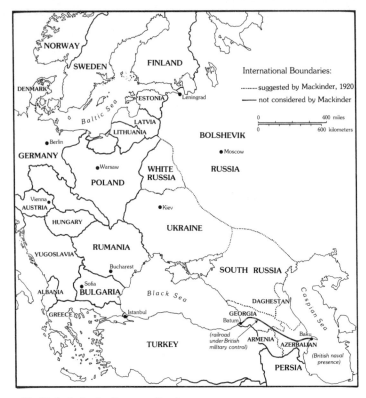

International Boundaries:

.... suggested by Mackinder, 1920

——— not considered by Mackinder

5 Mackinder's plan for European Russia, 1920.

German success against Russia in the First World War.

The British foreign secretary, Balfour, had wanted a Europe in which Germany and Russia had a common boundary; otherwise, without a mutual frontier, Germany would have more freedom of action in Western Europe and Russia could pursue policies in the Far East.[3] This was not the prevailing view in the Foreign Office, where the nationality principle was well established. French policy-makers wanted new states to serve as allies on Germany's eastern flank. Self-determination could be used to produce that result on the map.

The First World War was concluded with the following treaties. The treaty with Germany, signed at Versailles on 28 June 1919, contained the covenants of the League of Nations. The US Senate did not ratify the treaty. The treaty of St Germain (10

6 Boundaries of European states, *c.* 1922.

September 1919) made a peace with Austria. Under the treaty of Neuilly (21 November 1919) Bulgaria, an ally of the central powers, gave up territory to newly created Yugoslavia and lost the Aegean coastline it had held briefly before the war. Hungary signed the treaty of Trianon on 4 June 1920 giving up territory to Poland, Czechoslovakia, Austria, Romania and Yugoslavia.

The treaty of Sèvres (10 August 1920) with Turkey recognized independence for the Kurds and the Armenians, but was never ratified. After a war with Greece (1920–22), Turkey signed the treaty of Lausanne (24 July 1923), gave up territory inhabited by non-Turks and demilitarized the Straits leading from the Black Sea to the Mediterranean. After a short independence Armenia became a Soviet Socialist Republic. The Kurds did not get their state.

The first 26 articles of the treaty of Versailles contained the covenants of the League of Nations. Thirty-two countries comprised the original members, shortly joined by another thirteen. Although the League of Nations was a direct product of the peacemaking process, all the defeated powers were excluded from the League at the beginning. Nor was the Soviet Union a member. The League was based in Geneva and run by a Secretary General. There was an assembly and a council. Member states agreed to settle disputes by negotiation, and if one member attacked another it would be deemed 'to have committed an act of war against all other members of the League' (Article 16, Versailles). Robert Lansing, US Secretary of State, could not endorse Wilson's concept of a League empowered to use force,[4] and the Senate saw that the clause could drag the US into a war. The US never joined the League.

Much literature appearing after the war was hopeful in tone. Events proved the optimists wrong. Most of the commentators now reviewed saw the flaws in the new Europe and warned that war was on the way.

When we last encountered Halford Mackinder (1861–1947) lecturing at the Royal Geographical Society in 1904, he was teaching at the Oxford School of Geography and the London School of Economics, while dabbling in politics. In 1910 he was elected to Parliament as the Conservative and Unionist member for the Glasgow constituency of Camlachie. As the war came to an end Mackinder rapidly completed a book entitled *Democratic Ideals and Reality*, which was published in the spring of 1919.[5]

The war had revealed that the closed 'Heartland' of Eurasia was more extensive than Mackinder had suggested in 1904. Allied navies had been unable to penetrate the Baltic and Black Seas. From a strategic perspective the Heartland included the zones of internal drainage and Arctic drainage described in the pivot paper and, in addition, all the lands lying between the Black Sea and the Baltic, including the lower and middle Danube Valley. The war had shown that the strategic core of Eurasia was larger than suggested in the pivot paper and extended to include Central Europe, bringing within the bounds of the Heartland many additional resources, routeways and manufacturing regions (illus. 1).[6]

To contain the European margin of the Heartland, Mackinder proposed a 'Middle Tier' of states running from the Baltic to the Adriatic (illus. 4). Although the states were to be based on national groupings, which would have the effect of downsizing the great 'Kaiserdoms', devolving power away from Berlin, Vienna and Moscow, the main function of the Middle Tier would be to keep Eastern Europe out of the control of Germany and/or the Soviet Union. The First World War had started as a struggle between Germany and Russia for control of the region. The Middle Tier states would not be capable of performing a buffer function unless they were supported by the League of Nations. Here Mackinder issued his famous warning:

Who rules East Europe commands the Heartland:
Who rules the Heartland commands the World-Island:
Who rules the World-Island commands the World.[7]

Mackinder predicted that if the Middle Tier of states failed, there would be a war, in Eastern Europe, between Germany and the Soviet Union. For at least a generation the greatest threat would come from Germany.[8]

Mackinder was not solely concerned with territory. Repeatedly he wondered how long the world would remain a safe place for democracy and feared that the suppression of the safeguards of democracy, during the war, had allowed central governments to become too powerful.[9] Populations were half-educated. They could understand a slogan but had not formed the habit of analysing ideas. Politics was in danger of being taken over by ruthless organizers[10] who would control the apparatus of increasingly centralized states. Mackinder could have made more of this piece of prophesy for it was not long before dictators like Stalin, Mussolini, Hitler, and Franco started to take control of Europe. In fact, by 1939 all the states of Central and Eastern Europe were under the control of dictators.

Democratic Ideals and Reality was pessimistic and in 1919 it was criticized for being out of tune with the hopeful tendencies of the time. However, Mackinder had written a book that portrayed the coming of the Second World War and predicted the territorial issues over which it would start. Further, he sensed the coming of the totalitarian regimes that would bring the world to war.

ALBERT DEMANGEON AND THE DECLINE OF EUROPE

Albert Demangeon (1872–1940) was the leading French geographer of his generation. During the First World War he worked in the 'section géographique française', an organization that helped shape France's policies on territorial arrangements after the war. In 1920 Demangeon published *Le déclin de l'Europe*, which was translated into English and published in London. By the time the book appeared in the US the title had become *America and the Race for World Domination* (1921) for the theme of the book was that the US had advanced as Europe had declined.[11]

Demangeon's view was that the major states of Europe had exhausted themselves in the First World War. The region was in decay. The war had decreased agricultural output, reduced industrial capacity, diminished exports, created huge debts, reduced birth rates, and raised the average age of populations. As Europe was destroying itself the US and Japan had increased industrial capacity, taken over Europe's export markets and, as a result of shipping supplies to the belligerents, were owed huge debts by European countries.

Demangeon's figures were startling. Before the First World War France had 16 million acres in wheat. By 1918 only 10 million acres were in wheat cultivation and harvests had declined proportionately. The major cause of decline was the conscription of labour (farming was the largest employer in France) and at the end of the war there was not a rapid resurgence of agriculture, for many farm workers were killed or wounded in the war. Others did not return to rural areas.

European population numbers declined as a result of the war. France lost 1.4 million dead, Germany 2.1 million, and Britain suffered losses of nearly a million men. The war disrupted family life and birth rates fell so that, for example, there were 885,000 more deaths than births in Germany in 1918. The usual postwar baby boom was not going to result in a demographic rebound for the age structure of populations had been altered. During the war France lost one in five of all the men aged 20–44! Postwar population numbers were static and the population was ageing. In Germany, after the war, in the age group 20–30 there were 1,230 women to every thousand men.[12]

The figures for trade, shipping and finance showed how Europe had given up leadership to the US and Japan.[13] In 1914 the value of US exports to all parts of the world exceeded imports by $435 million. By 1918 the excess of exports over imports was $3,567,000,000! In the twelve months ending 30 June 1918 the value of US exports to Europe reached $5,928,000,000. Few goods were shipped from Europe to the US as European industries were engaged in the war. The result of the one-way trade was a torrent of currency, gold and IOU's leaving Europe for the US. The leadership of the financial world shifted from London and the pound to New York and the dollar.

Overall, Japanese exports, from a lower base grew, more rapidly than those of the US, as Japanese manufacturers took over markets formerly supplied by European factories.[14] Japanese and US merchant fleets grew rapidly. In 1914 the US built just over 200,000 tons of merchant ships. In 1918 the figure was nearly 4 million tons. In 1914 US shipbuilding output was one-seventh of that of the UK. By 1918 the US was launching three times the tonnage of the UK.[15] The story was the same in other industries. In 1913 the US produced 24 million tons of steel; by 1918, the figure was 45 million tons. The US chemical industry, insulated from German competition, was able to make a greater range of products and move into export markets.

Japan also achieved spectacular percentage gains in industrial output, exports and shipbuilding. Japanese shipping lines were coming to dominate Pacific routes and, although it would not be recognized until later, the *Zaibatsu* (money cliques) were beginning to ensure that all trade with Japan was carried in ships built, owned and operated by Japanese combines.[16]

Beyond Europe, Demangeon saw that the European empires were vulnerable, as the 'native races' were awakening politically.[17] Conflict was coming between the Islamic regions and the civilization of Europe. Japan was about to promote a racial doctrine of 'Asia for the Asiatics' and would create a circle of influence by 'conquest or by commerce' in the region.

In *Le déclin de l'Europe* Demangeon did not propose any solutions to Europe's problems. Later in the decade he called for the creation of a European bloc as a means of unifying the region and increasing economic interaction. The French foreign minister, Briand, embraced the idea and carried it to the League of Nations.[18]

ISAIAH BOWMAN AND THE NEW WORLD

In 1915, at the age of 37, Isaiah Bowman was appointed to the directorship of the American Geographical Society in New York. As the US was drawn into the First World War, Bowman helped the so-called Inquiry, which eventually moved into the American Geographical Society premises and which created a store of information on all aspects of the geography of Europe, including mapping the distribution of national, ethnic and linguistic groups. At the end of hostilities, the Inquiry was disbanded but Bowman was appointed Chief Territorial Specialist of the American Commission to Negotiate the Peace and accompanied President Wilson to France on board the USS *Washington*.[19] During the making of the treaties Bowman was closely involved in the details concerning postwar boundaries. On return to the US he wrote *The New World: Problems in Political Geography* (1921),[20] which was acknowledged to be an important study of world affairs. The Department of State ordered several hundred copies and placed them in US consular offices around the world.

On the surface, Bowman's book is a detached, rational analysis of the problems of countries and regions in the postwar world. From another perspective the book is an indictment of the peacemaking process and the problems it had created. Bowman, the territorial specialist, was appalled at the number of new boundaries created in Europe. Far from seeing self-determination as a sacred principle he thought it would cause problems. People of different cultural groups were not neatly divided on the ground, and clean boundary-making between ethnic groups was not practical.[21] Problems could not be solved by splitting up the world indefinitely. Every ethnic group could not have its own flag and place in the family of nations. The solution was to have guaranteed rights of free speech and religion for minorities within countries.

And the man who had been taken to Paris specifically to help with boundary issues made this observation:

> ... war may come, not in a generation, but in a few years. The danger spots of the world have been greatly increased in number, the zones of friction lengthened. Where there were approximately 8,000 miles of old boundary about the former states of central Europe, there are now 10,000 miles, and of this total more than 3,000 miles represent newly located boundaries. Every additional mile of new boundary, each new location, has increased for a time the sources of possible trouble between unlike and, in the main, unfriendly peoples.[22]

The statement was not meant solely as criticism of the peace treaties for in Bowman's view the world was broken, international life disrupted, and people were, in general, motivated by personal gain in a world that was 'disorganized, unstable, and dangerous'. Bowman believed that many postwar problems resulted from a peace made as the world fell into disorder.[23]

Bowman identified other problems. Religion was still a major force. Islam would become more militant in the Middle East, Africa, and the Indian subcontinent. Like Mackinder, Bowman was wary of mass political movements and particularly the spread of Bolshevism.

Bowman admired the trade connections of the British Empire but in taking on mandates in the Middle East, the empire was overextending itself. France faced economic and demographic stagnation and the gap between France and Germany would widen again.[24] German losses of territory, resources and productive capacity were large. Germany lost the Saar and Silesia. The Saar had produced 9 per cent of German coal and Silesia 20 per cent. The merchant marine had been lost in the war or confiscated at the end. The German populations detached, or excluded, from the country would give trouble in the future. Overall Germany would work through the economic difficulties but Bowman doubted the country would achieve political stability.[25]

The new states of Europe did not have a secure future. Landlocked Czechoslovakia had boundary disputes with all five neighbours and the Slovaks would break away.[26] They did in 1939 and 1993. Practically every mile of the Yugoslav frontiers bordered an unfriendly country and, because of the large number of ethnic groups within the state, Bowman doubted it was viable.[27] There were three Polands: German Poland centred on Posen; Russian Poland focused on Warsaw; and Austrian or Galician Poland looked to Kraków and Przemyś.[28] The boundaries of the state were difficult to defend and there was the problem of establishing friendly relations with Germany and the Soviet Union. In Bowman's view it was doubtful that the Soviet Union would hold together.

After the war Bowman helped found the Council on Foreign Relations and served on the editorial board of *Foreign Affairs*.[29] He became president of Johns Hopkins University (1935–48) and was an advisor to President Roosevelt and the State Department in the Second World War. Bowman was an important part of the collective memory that ensured that some mistakes made at the end of the First World War were not repeated at the end of the Second World War.

GENERAL KARL HAUSHOFER AND
GERMAN *GEOPOLITIK*

As the First World War ended, Mackinder drafted *Democratic Ideals and Reality*, Bowman worked at the Inquiry, and Demangeon studied European boundary problems. Karl Haushofer (1869–1946), a professional soldier, was still with his Bavarian regiment on the Western front. Between 1908 and 1910 he had served as a military observer in Japan and on return to Germany published *Dai Nihon* (1913), a book describing the rising military and economic power of Japan. The following year he received a doctoral degree at Munich University.[30] Haushofer retired from the military in 1919, with the rank of Major-General, and began a new career in Munich lecturing and writing on geopolitics.

Before we examine Haushofer's role as a purveyor of *Geopolitik* let us look, following Daniel Deudney, at the general premises of German geopolitics.[31] Deudney identified six major themes:

1. 'The primary political entities are states and states are organisms.'

2. The success of states is dependent upon *Lebensraum* – living space.

3. States compete for space. Successful states expand and occupy additional space at the expense of weaker states.

4. States strive for autarky. That is, states strive to produce all required materials, goods, and services within the territory of the state. This implies statist policies to make optimum use of resources.

5. As states are natural organisms, 'their actions are beyond right and wrong'.

6. In the industrial age the optimum size of states will grow, leading to competition between states to control earth space.

The reader will recognize that all of the above is explicit, or implicit, in the work of Ratzel. General Haushofer used these themes in developing ideas about German expansion and is regarded as the most influential of the German geopoliticians in the interwar period, but there were many other contributors to *Geopolitik*. A wide-ranging review of German geopoliticians is provided by David Thomas Murphy in *The Heroic Earth: Geopolitical Thought in Weimar Germany 1918–1933*. The geopolitik school made extensive use of sketches and diagrams to illustrate policy objectives.[32]

Like most Germans, Karl Haushofer was disturbed by the New Europe that emerged out of the First World War. Many trends of the preceding half century, favourable to Germany, had been halted. The unification of Germany had been partially undone by the Polish corridor. The notion that all Germans would become part of a greater *Deutschland* was set back. German-speaking communities were in the new states of Czechoslovakia and Poland. Alsace and Lorraine had reverted to France. The Austrians were forbidden union with Germany by the treaty of Versailles.

The creation of a *Mitteleuropa*, dominated by Germany, had apparently been stalled by the formation of a tier of East European states that ran from the Baltic to the Adriatic. The tier was designed to prevent *Drang nach Osten*, although in a decade it was to facilitate German penetration. German ambitions to be a world power had been suppressed by the confiscation of colonies and the limitations placed upon land, air and naval forces.

Karl Haushofer began to construct in his writings a new world order in which some of the injustices of the peace treaties would be corrected, and Germany would return to a prominent place in European and world affairs. In Haushofer's view the problems could only be solved by German expansion and the creation of more *Lebensraum*, so that Germany would control *Mitteleuropa* and create a greater *Deutschland*.[33]

By 1924 Haushofer was making an impact. In that year, he published *Geopolitik des Pazifischen Ocean* and began to edit *Zeitschrift für Geopolitik*. Overall he would publish 40 books and hundreds of articles. Like most German geopoliticians he subscribed to ideas of *Lebensraum*. Haushofer's concept of *Lebensraum* was linked to his vision of *Deutschland*. *Deutschland* was not simply the territory occupied by the German state but all lands settled by people of German speech and culture. Karl Haushofer wanted the people of German stock united within a German state and was active in *Volksdeutsche* organizations which worked to bring this about.[34]

In 1925 Haushofer set out those borderland areas which he thought were part of the German system.[35] The list includes North Schleswig, which had chosen to become part of Denmark by plebiscite in 1920, Eupen-Malmédy, which had been attached to Belgium by the treaty of Versailles, the Saar, separated from Germany in 1920 and returned by plebiscite in 1935, Alsace and Lorraine, Austria, the Tyrol, Moravia, parts of Poland, Danzig, Memelland, and the lands occupied by Germans, in the Danube valley beyond Austria.

Notice that most of the territorial claims involved the creation of Haushofer's *Deutschland* and the unification of the *Volksdeutsche* within an enlarged German state. Unlike Hitler, Haushofer did not want to take over lands occupied by Slavs and looked for an alliance with the Soviet Union. Later he was to alter his views to suit the situation.

Haushofer referred to Halford Mackinder's work as the greatest of all world views and adapted Mackinder's Heartland thesis to his own needs. Following Mackinder, Haushofer saw a conflict developing between the oceanic empires – the 'space-owning imperialists' in the general's phrase – and the oppressed continental powers.[36] The main enemy for Germany was the British empire.[37] In the struggle between land power and sea power Haushofer thought he saw how Germany could emerge a winner. Following Mackinder he suggested an alliance with the Soviet Union so that the vast resources of Eurasia could be used to support German ambitions on the world scene.

If you are bent on world domination that is one scenario to be played out in war games. However, in a land power vs. sea power struggle it is not certain where the interests of Germany lie. As Hugill points out countries like France and Germany have two realms – a marine, mercantile element represented by ports such as Bordeaux and Hamburg and the territorial interiors 'which generate wealth through the occupation and exploitation of territory and are thus disposed to militarism'.[38] Mackinder made a similar point in 1919. Germany got into a two-front war because it failed to choose between the maritime world of the Hamburg merchant and the territorial Germany that had traditionally sought *Lebensraum* in the east.

Both Hitler and Haushofer understood the two-front problem. For Haushofer the answer was to make a deal with Russia and expand at the expense of the space-owning imperialists. Hitler saw the obverse. Subdue France in the west and drive to the east.[39] As *Mein Kampf* (1927) states, 'the strength of our nation is founded, not on colonies, but on the soil of our European homeland'.[40] At the Nürnburg party rally of 1936 more specifics were given:

If the Urals with their incalculable wealth of raw materials, the rich forests of Siberia, and the unending cornfields of the Ukraine lay within Germany … the country would swim in plenty.[41]

Haushofer thought the way to achieve German aims was via alliances with the Soviet Union and Japan. Hitler saw the value of Japan as a counterweight to communism and as a threat to the US in the Pacific. But there is consistency to Hitler's view that Germany should acquire land in the east, at the expense of the Soviet Union.[42]

Haushofer made use of the concept of pan regions – the division of earth space into major units, or spheres of influence, in which one power was dominant. The number and boundaries of Haushofer's pan regions varied. For example, one version of his views in 1931 had four major regions – America, Eurafrica, Pan Russia and Pan Asia.[43] By 1941 he was down to three regions: Americas (dominated by the US), Eurafrica (dominated by Germany) and Asia (dominated by Japan). In Haushofer's schemes, Britain and France, together with their empires, were in the Euro region dominated by Germany.[44]

Hitler's mental map differed from that of Haushofer concerning pan regions. Throughout the 1930s, and even after the war started, in Hitler's mind, the British empire occupied a major segment of earth space.[45] We can debate the length of time the empire would have survived had Germany conquered Europe from the Atlantic to the Urals but here again is a difference of view between Hitler and Haushofer.

The question arises as to what influence Haushofer had upon Hitler and upon German foreign policy between the wars. Haushofer met Hess in 1919 and Hitler later. Hess attended the general's lectures and when Hess and Hitler were imprisoned at Landsberg, following the Beer Hall *Putsch*, Haushofer visited them between 24 June and 12 November 1924. At this time Hitler was exposed to the views of Ratzel, Kjellén and Haushofer.[46] The general tutored Hitler and Hess and had them read *Politische Geographie* by Ratzel and Haushofer's *Dai Nihon*, especially material dealing with a potential alliance between Japan, Russia and Germany.

Undoubtedly Haushofer taught but what did the students absorb and believe? Stoakes argues that some of Hitler's foreign policy notions may be traced to Heinrich Class and Hitler's association with the DAP, the forerunner of the Nazi party.[47] Whatever the influences, *Mein Kampf* exhibits the

Geopolitik style. For example, Hitler wrote:

> The foreign policy of the folkish state must safeguard the existence ... of the race embodied in the state, by creating a healthy, viable natural relation between the nation's population and growth on the one hand and the quantity and quality of its soil on the other hand.[48]

Is this based on Haushofer, Ratzel or a folkish tradition that predates Ratzel?

Haushofer did take part in foreign policy. In 1923 he was involved in secret talks between Germany, Japan and the USSR.[49] Over a period of time, due to his knowledge of the Pacific world, Haushofer was able to bring Germany and Japan closer together. He was involved with Munich and, over the years, the general gave advice to Hess and occasionally Hitler.[50] Haushofer could not alter Hitler's view of eastward expansion, which resulted in Operation Barbarossa in 1941, but as the battle progressed he gave support to Hitler and the campaign in his publications.

Perhaps Haushofer was most useful as a publicist. After 1933 *Zeitschrift für Geopolitik* was selling nearly 700,000 copies a year. Haushofer's articles were widely published in newspapers and he delivered radio talks. He spread many of the ideas concerning *Lebensraum*, autarky and German expansion which formed the basis of Nazi foreign policy, and these notions found their way into school texts.[51]

At the end of the war Karl Haushofer was interrogated as a potential defendant at the war crimes trials. One of the statements he made can be read in Edmund Walsh's *Total Power*.[52] To Walsh the general represented himself as a misunderstood academic. He had some publications, for example *Dai Nihon*, which were respected. Holger Herwig reveals the other side of Haushofer as a servant of the Nazi party in propagating ideas concerning *Lebensraum* and Nazi psychology. However, Haushofer wanted to expand the German state until it included the German populations of Central Europe. This is different from Hitler who wished to extend German living space, while 'cleansing the earth' of Jews, Slavs and Gypsies to make way for Nordic settlers.

Among the elements that saved General Haushofer from the war crimes court were the facts that he had spent time in Dachau and that his son Albrecht, who was connected with peace movements and plots against Hitler, was murdered by the Gestapo as the war ended. Karl Haushofer and his wife Martha, who had helped with so many of the books, committed suicide in 1946.

Hector Bywater (1884–1940) was born in London but spent much of his early life in the US, Canada, West Africa and Germany. He spoke German fluently. In 1904 he covered the Russo-Japanese war for the *New York Herald* and built up a successful career in journalism, writing for newspapers and magazines in the UK and the US. He became expert on the naval build-up prior to the First World War and spent much time in Germany writing articles and sending intelligence reports to the British Admiralty.[53] During the First World War he worked in intelligence in Britain and then resumed his career as author and journalist.

Bywater covered the Washington Naval Conference (1920–21) and at first in newspaper reports welcomed the effort to limit naval armaments. However, the agreements contained clauses that prevented further fortification of Pacific island naval bases. Bywater recognized that this stipulation made the US positions in the Philippines and Guam vulnerable to attack by Japan. When he published *Seapower in the Pacific* (1921), Bywater described the Pacific problem:

> When the United States relieved Spain of the Philippines she gave hostages to fortune in a sense which the American people have never fully realized. But for the acquisition of these islands [the US] need never have maintained a powerful fleet in the Pacific ... their possession, however, at once advanced the frontiers of the United States nearly 7,000 miles across the Pacific and made her an Asiatic Power, thereby conferring upon her all the cares and responsibilities inseparable from that status.[54]

The bases in the Philippines were not fortified and did not have the facilities to repair, maintain and supply a fleet. Japanese invasion of the islands would present no serious difficulty. The naval base at Hawaii was 5,000 miles from the Philippines. Naval bases in Japan were 1,300–1,750 miles from the islands. If the Japanese attacked the Philippines, their flag would be flying over Manila by the time the US fleet arrived. The US fleet would be far from bases and could not sustain a prolonged campaign.[55]

Although the naval base at Pearl Harbor was well situated to defend the Pacific Coast of the US, it was too far from the Philippines to provide support. The key to the situation was Guam. The island, lying less than 1,500 nautical miles east of Manila, needed fortification. If Guam was secured as a base no force would dare attack the Philippines. Conversely, the Japanese could successfully attack an undefended Guam[56] and could then take the Philippines at their leisure, certain that no US force could interfere with them.[57]

Bywater warned that the Japanese were likely to attack without warning. In 1894 a Japanese naval squadron began hostilities against China a week before the declaration of war and the Russians had been attacked at Port Arthur (1904) a few hours after negotiations broke down. In December 1941 the Japanese declaration of war was to arrive after the attack on Pearl Harbor.

Bywater concluded that:

> The enormous expanse of the Pacific makes base power and large steaming radius the dominating factors in the strategical problems of that ocean. Without a chain of well-defended fuel stations it would be impossible for the American Fleet to operate for any length of time in the Western Pacific.[58]

Looking back, the need for the US fleet to have well-defended bases for operations on the far side of the Pacific seems obvious. That was not conventional wisdom in 1920. As Honan argues, Mahan had lectured at the Naval War College on the need to concentrate, not disperse, forces. For Mahan naval strength was not the possession of strategic strong points but rather of a mobile, concentrated, fleet. Too many bases involved scattering fighting ships to protect the bases.

Both American and Japanese planners accepted Mahan's view, and it was assumed that the Japanese would not want to disperse forces either. Bywater perceived that the Japanese could seize the Philippines and Guam, and then concentrate the fleet to repel any counter-attack.[59]

Unfortunately, the United States in the Five Power Naval Treaty (1922) agreed, along with Britain, Japan, France and Italy, to a clause on Insular Possessions in the Pacific which precluded further fortification. Hawaii was excluded, but the Philippines and Guam were left unprotected.[60]

COUDENHOVE-KALERGI AND THE EUROPEAN UNION

Count Richard Nicolaus Coudenhove-Kalergi (1894–1972) was a product of a cosmopolitan family. In the eighteenth century part of the Coudenhove family left Brabant for Germany. Prosperity followed and Richard's grandfather married a daughter of the Kalergi family from Crete. Richard's father Heinrich (1859–1906) came from that union and he entered the diplomatic service of Austria-Hungary, working in Athens, Rio, Constantinople, Buenos Aires and Tokyo, where he served as Chargé d'affaires and married Mitsou Ooyama. When Count Heinrich inherited the family estates and left the diplomatic service, he settled at Castle Ronsperg, in Bohemia, and studied linguistics and philosophy. He gained a doctorate from the University of Prague, with a dissertation on anti-Semitism which became the basis of a book.[61] Count Heinrich, a Catholic, also wrote on the need for equality and tolerance within Austria-Hungary and on the role of the empire as a bridge between the Germanic and Slav lands. Heinrich mastered sixteen languages and found the time to tutor his children in Russian and Hungarian.

Count Richard Coudenhove-Kalergi was brought up at Ronsperg before being educated in Vienna where he completed a doctoral degree. Coudenhove-Kalergi was appalled by the way Europe had been devastated by the war. The conflict had settled nothing and regional cooperation was further away than ever. In the case of Austria-Hungary, an economic community was destroyed as the customs union and common currency died with the empire.

In 1923, Count Coudenhove-Kalergi founded the Pan European Union with the aim of creating a United States of Europe. Coudenhove-Kalergi had a strong sense that Europe was a cultural entity, not a physical geographical unit, for it was only a peninsula of the Eurasian continent.[62] Within the eastern boundaries of Europe were Finland, the Baltic states, Poland, Czechoslovakia, Hungary and Romania. Europe did not extend to the Urals. Historically, Russia had been a threat to Europe. The Soviet Union was not a democracy and should not be included in the European Union.

Like Demangeon, Coudenhove-Kalergi thought that Europe had ceased to be the centre of the world, and that the US had become the leading power. Coudenhove-Kalergi had a strong strategic vision, believing that Russia would re-emerge as a powerful force, and threaten Europe.[63] Out of the Russian Revolution would 'emerge a Russian Napoleon' who would take over the newly created petty states of East Europe as a stepping stone to the domination of all Europe. The Austro-Hungarian and German empires had been barriers to Russian territorial ambitions.[64] The war had destroyed Austria-Hungary and weakened Germany. In place of the military monarchies of Central Europe stood half a dozen medium- and small-sized states. Poland and Romania were not going to take the place of Austria and Prussia as a counterweight to Russia. To avoid Russian domination, Coudenhove-Kalergi urged that all the European states – from Poland to Portugal – be consolidated politically and economically.[65]

There are similarities between the strategic views of Coudenhove-Kalergi and Halford Mackinder. Both saw East Europe as weak, and control of East Europe as key to the dominance of Europe. Mackinder feared Germany more than Russia, and Germany did become the first threat to East Europe at the beginning of the Second World War. Coudenhove-Kalergi feared Russia more than Germany, and the Soviet Union did take over East Europe after the Second World War. Both feared a German–Russian alliance. Coudenhove-Kalergi thought that if Germany was not bound into Europe, a German–Russian alliance was only a matter of time[66] with Europe being roughly divided along the Rhine. The German–Soviet Non Aggression Pact of 1939 put some aspects of this scenario in place.

Coudenhove-Kalergi saw the problems of creating a Europe that was politically and economically united. The central difficulty was overcoming the antagonism between France and Germany.[67] Then there was the problem of Britain. How was Britain to be fitted into the European structure? Was Britain destined to be the mediator between North America and Europe without belonging to either? In any event, Britain was not likely to be part of Europe until the British empire was dissolved.

Both Coudenhove-Kalergi and Demangeon saw Britain as having to make a choice between Europe and Empire. Neither suggested that France, also with an overseas empire, had to make a similar choice. A map in Coudenhove-Kalergi (1926) shows a pan Europe that includes the French overseas territories.[68]

Economically, Coudenhove-Kalergi saw that the postwar new Europe, created at Paris, was not made for cooperation. The many new frontiers and customs barriers were a hindrance to trade. Germany was divided by the Danzig corridor and the German economic system damaged by the loss of Alsace-Lorraine (iron ore and potash), Upper Silesia (coal and steel) and the Saar (coal). The Austro-Hungarian economic system had been dismembered. The industrialized Czech lands were cut off from former markets by tariffs. Vienna, once a European capital serving 50 million people, had been severed from its hinterland. It was now a shrinking city with declining numbers, high unemployment and food shortages.

The First World War had fragmented Europe and destroyed any cooperative economic structures that had existed. It would not be easy to create the European Union that Coudenhove-Kalergi wanted. He felt war was more likely, and believed that Europe was rushing headlong towards hostilities, with most states in Central and East Europe already preparing for the next fight.

Coudenhove-Kalergi had an idea of a European Union stretching from Portugal to Poland that is now being approached. His long-term vision was complemented by a grasp of short-term realities. The threat from Russia, the fear of a German–Soviet alliance, the intractable nature of the French–German rivalry, were forces that would play themselves out before a European community emerged.

Coudenhove-Kalergi's ideas were not ignored. In 1926 he met Amery in London, who recorded in his diary a lunch argument with Churchill over the merits of *Pan Europe*, with Winston taking Coudenhove-Kalergi's position, declaring that the pivot of world peace would be a combination of Britain, France and Germany.[69] Both Amery and Churchill were to write introductions to books by Coudenhove-Kalergi.

Count Richard published prolifically but most of his output was in German and not translated into English. By the mid 1930s the war that he had predicted was arriving and in *The Totalitarian State*, which was translated into English, he saw that the idea of the state as a living thing, an organism, would completely undermine the rights of individuals.[70] Further he made a distinction between fascism and National Socialism. Mussolini's fascism was about creating a 'corporative state' and Count Richard did not disapprove of that[71] but National Socialism proceeded from a 'mystic biological conception of race, from the belief in a common Aryan bloodstream, creating a common national body of all Germans which no artificial frontiers can divide'.[72]

The commentators reviewed in this chapter – Mackinder, Demangeon, Bowman, Haushofer, Bywater and Coudenhove-Kalergi – could all claim to have predicted events. Bowman warned that war would come in a few years; it did. Mackinder predicted that East Europe would be the ground on which the battle for the Heartland would start; it was. Bywater predicted accurately that Japan would attack US positions in the Pacific. He did not name Pearl Harbor but he warned of an attack before the declaration of war.

Haushofer could claim from 1938 until the midsummer of 1941 that his policies were being followed. Like many Germans, he looked to Hitler to right the wrongs of Versailles but found that the Führer's ambitions outdistanced their own and brought defeat on the road to the Urals.

Coudenhove-Kalergi saw it all. A war was coming and out of the ruins there would be a chance to build a united Europe, capable of resisting Russia. He underestimated the role of the US but today Europe looks much as he hoped. Count Richard Coudenhove-Kalergi was nominated, unsuccessfully, for the Nobel Peace Prize in 1949. The man who kept alive the idea of European unity in the 1920s and 1930s when events were pulling Europe apart is largely forgotten. His ideas were heard and echoed in France in the 1920s and it was France, after the Second World War, that promoted the concept of a European Community.

Coudenhove-Kalergi was not alone in proposing schemes of international cooperation;[73] they have appeared in large numbers in the twentieth century. Leading British statesmen like Churchill were interested in the concept of a united Europe but uninterested in the details, although L. S. Amery did attend Coudenhove-Kalergi's third pan-European conference in Basle in 1932.[74] Amery suggested a loosely integrated Europe along the lines of the British Commonwealth and there were other British commentators who wanted to create a federation of European states.[75] But this tradition, born of thinking about bringing the Commonwealth closer together, was not actively developed by British statesmen after the Second World War as a model for European unity.

It is no coincidence that Count Richard was from Austria-Hungary. The empire was promoting a community that in economic form was similar to that which emerged in Western Europe, with a customs union, shared economic space, a central bank and a common currency. Several prominent men and women from Austria-Hungary who had experienced the collapse of that multiethnic empire helped to keep the idea of a broader European community alive. For example, the Hungarian-born Emery Reves (1904–1981) established a press agency in 1930. Articles were commissioned from statesmen, translated into several languages and syndicated in newspapers across Europe to disseminate ideas within the region.[76]

Coudenhove-Kalergi and Reves would have agreed with Bowman that you could not split up the world indefinitely and give every group a state. The way forward was the constitutional guarantee of equality, freedom of speech and freedom of religion to all men and women. But constitutional guarantees of individual liberties were not on the minds of the totalitarian regimes that were about to dominate Europe.

FOUR

The Collapse of World Order

The Europe that emerged after the First World War lacked coherence. The new, multinational states had problems with borders, neighbours and minorities and lacked viable economies, stable political institutions, foreign currency reserves and established machinery of government. There were manufacturing industries in Czechoslovakia at Prague, Pilsen and Brno and in Polish Silesia, but most of East Europe was agricultural, with farming being the dominant form of employment, often on large estates owned by the landowning elite.

Perhaps if Europe had rebounded after the war, economic growth would have corrected problems. But Europe, as a whole, was in debt and new states had to repay old debts. Czechoslovakia got a share of Austrian debt and the responsibility to pay a part of the reparations bill laid on the central powers. All across Europe, money that might have been used for investment and the revitalization of economic life was used to pay war debts in one form or another. Eventually, the debts helped the global economic system into the Great Depression, as Keynes had predicted and tried to prevent.[1]

The fragile economies of East Europe were not helped by events. In January 1923 France and Belgium sent troops into the Ruhr in a futile attempt to extract reparations. Much German industry closed down and the country accelerated into a hyper-inflation that made the mark, savings, government bonds, pensions, insurance policies and fixed incomes worthless.[2] Economic problems in Germany meant decreased markets for the agricultural products and industrial raw materials which the new states exported.

Efforts were made to lessen tensions. In 1925 at Locarno on the Swiss shore of Lake Maggiore the European powers met in an attempt to promote harmony. Germany agreed to accept her boundaries with France and Belgium as set out in the treaty of Versailles. Britain and France agreed to remove their Rhine forces on a more rapid timetable than laid down at Versailles. Germany agreed to leave the Rhineland demilitarized and joined the League of Nations.

In 1928 the US, France, Germany, Britain, Italy, Japan and some 60 other nations signed the Kellogg-Briand pact agreeing to avoid war as a means of settling disputes. The US Secretary of State, Kellogg, received the Nobel Peace Prize in 1929 but the sentiments of the pact had a short life. The stock market crash of 1929 led to the undermining of the US economy and in the Depression that followed, world trade shrank by 60 per cent. Things were made worse by the intensification of protectionist policies. Smoot-Hawley (1930) increased tariffs on imports to the US. In 1932 the UK adopted a tariff system giving prefer- ence to goods entering Britain from Commonwealth countries. In the same year Germany raised tariffs on imports while giving favourable treatment to Hungary, in an effort to expand influ- ence in southeast Europe. Countries were trying to insulate against world market forces and in Europe economists began to publish extensively on the theory of autarky – the creation of self-sufficient economic units that were independent of world- wide economic shifts,[3] the antithesis of free trade and globalization. The aim of autarky is to produce, within the terri- tory of the state, all the foodstuffs, raw materials and manufactured goods required by the state and its inhabitants. If a country lacked basic manufacturing activities then the state should intervene to promote new industries. Raw material shortages could be corrected by bi-lateral trade agreements or by acquiring territory. Autarky requires state control of a wide range of economic activities and is attractive to dictatorial regimes. By 1930 Europe was falling into the grip of strong men – Pilsudski in Poland (1926), Mussolini in Italy (1928), Salazar, a professional economist, in Portugal (1932) and Hitler in Germany (1933). By 1936 all the new states of mainland Europe, with the exception of Czechoslovakia, were in the con- trol of dictatorial governments. The Soviet Union had been under a totalitarian regime since the end of the war and, with the start of the first five-year plan in 1928, was aiming for autarky.

Policies of autarky usually had popular support for they were seen as a way out of the Depression and a means of creating employment. To many fascism was about discipline, order, service to country and working to restore national vitality. Others were sympathetic to communism for the Soviet Union was apparently avoiding the economic chaos of free market capitalism. Both Stalin and Hitler strove for autarky.

The economic theory of autarky and the idea of a European *Großraumwirtshaft* (large economic area) was worked out before Hitler came to power. We have already encountered this form of economic thinking with Hollweg's European Economic Association and the shared, protected economic space of Austria-Hungary. When the Nazi party took power in Germany it did not have a detailed economic policy but it was committed to *Lebensraum*. As we have seen (chapter 3) autarky is implicit in *Lebensraum* and very quickly Nazi policy accepted the need for self-sufficiency (illus. 7).[4]

Germany has a good, but not complete, resource base. The coalfields, including the Ruhr, are rich. Iron deposits are limited but Sweden was a reliable supplier. Germany coveted the ores of Lorraine but these are not as valuable as the igneous Swedish ores, with an iron content in excess of 60 per cent. The Luxembourg and Lorraine ores are in sedimentary rock, have a low iron content and require a different smelting technology. Zinc, lead, copper and potash were produced within Germany but she needed to import oil, manganese, nickel, tungsten and other non-ferrous metals. Synthetics were filling some gaps. During the First World War nitrogen was fixed from the atmosphere to provide raw material for explosives and fertilizer. Gasoline products could be distilled from coal, at a price, and synthetic rubber (*buna*) had been developed.

Germany was a net importer of live animals, meats and fats. This is only a cause for concern if you crave autarky, for the German market was supplied with ham, poultry, dairy products and livestock from Belgium, the Netherlands and Denmark. Compared with Holland and Denmark, German agriculture was inefficient. Far more produce could have been obtained from German soil if the government had promoted scientific farming but leading Nazis were engulfed in a myth of

7 Cartoon of June 25, 1941, by Dr Seuss. University of California, San Diego, Mandeville Special Collections Library (Dr. Seuss Collection).

Lebensraum leading to lands of plenty.

In theory the Soviet Union had the resource base to create an autarkic economy. Many of the resources lay in regions away from the major population centres in European Russia but under the five-year plans the Volga was harnessed for hydroelectric power and heavy industries constructed in towns along its banks. The exploitation of metallic ores in the Urals was increased as new towns, mines and smelters were created in the region. The Trans-Siberian railroad was improved and the great coalfield at Kuznetsk, in the heart of Siberia, was opened up. Iron and steel works were built there and ore brought in along the railway from the Urals to feed the steel mills, with return trains carrying coal to metal smelters in Ural towns like Magnitogorsk. The opening up of remote regions was partially driven by strategic considerations. However, existing industrial regions in the USSR were expanded, notably in the Ukraine, where the Don basin had the best raw material base for steelmaking in Europe. Iron ore, coal and limestone were abundant and not far away, at Nikopol, were deposits of manganese, a widely used hardening element in steel.[5]

There has always been a strong element of self-sufficiency in the French economy and although there was no formal policy of autarky France favoured trade patterns that limited imports and the outflow of currency. Her largest trading partner was the colony of Algeria, where trade was in francs. Caribbean, African and Asian colonies provided tropical products including strategically important rubber from southeast Asia. France did not produce enough coal, even with the Saar region. Britain was France's largest supplier of coal, followed by Germany.

For Italy, even under a fascist regime, autarky was a hopeless target. The country lacked sufficient coal, iron ore and oil. Most non-ferrous metals were imported. Italy did not produce enough wheat and the policies designed to correct that resulted in land being converted to cereals rather than higher-value fruit and vegetables. Central planning did deliver benefits such as an improved rail system and elimination of marshlands to create farmland and reduce malaria. State corporations took over private companies, including Alfa Romeo.[6]

Historically the cities of Italy had been commercial and manufacturing centres dependent upon long-distance trade and resources brought in from other countries. Mussolini wanted an increased maritime role for Italy, starting with control of the Mediterranean – *Mare Nostrum*. Mussolini resented the influence of Britain and France and the fact that the Royal Navy controlled the exits to the Mediterranean at Gibraltar and Suez. If Italy aligned with Britain and France she safeguarded her position in the Mediterranean. In 1935 the three powers met at Stresa, on the Italian shore of Lake Maggiore, in an effort to keep the First World War allies on the same side. But Mussolini thought that an alliance with Germany gave him a good chance of gaining Nice, Corsica, Tunis and Malta. The Italian colonies at Tripolitanea and Cyrenica could be used as a base for thrusts to the Atlantic, Suez and the Red Sea.[7]

The steps to war came quickly. In 1935 Hitler renounced the armament limitation clauses of Versailles. In October Italy attacked Ethiopia and was declared the aggressor by the League. In March 1936 Germany put troops into the Rhineland and remilitarized the region, in contravention of the treaty of Versailles and German undertakings negotiated at Locarno in 1925.

The remilitarization of the Rhineland altered the strategic geography of Europe. Instead of a neutral zone between France and Germany, there were German forces on the borders of Belgium and France. In place of German armies having to cross the Rhine from east to west, at a few bridging points, with the deployment problems that would pose in wartime, German troops could be grouped close to the borders of the Netherlands, Luxembourg, Belgium and France. The position of the Middle Tier states was weakened. German remilitarization of the Rhineland reduced France's ability to enter Germany, advance to the Rhine and threaten the Ruhr, Cologne and Frankfurt, if France's allies in the east were attacked.[8] In 1938 France found she had no option but war if she wanted to support Czechoslovakia against Germany.

In November 1936 Mussolini declared the existence of the Rome–Berlin Axis and the following year Italy withdrew from the League and joined Germany in the Anti-Comintern pact, aimed at the Soviet Union. In the meantime Japan occupied Manchuria (1932) and started large-scale campaigns in 1937 against China attacking Peking, Tientsin, Shanghai and Nanking.

In the spring of 1938 German forces entered Austria and the union of Germany and Austria (*Anschluss*) was declared on 13 March. The strategic implications were considerable, for Germany and Italy were now contiguous. The Axis ran from the shores of the Baltic and North Seas, across the Alps to the Mediterranean. The Italian colonies in Libya projected the Axis, via peninsular Italy, into Africa.

With the absorption of Austria, Germany became a Danubian power and acquired the river ports of Linz and Vienna. Vienna gave access to the Danubian plains. Downstream lay Budapest, Belgrade and the Black Sea. In the spring of 1938 it was too early to speak of Berlin to Baghdad, but Berlin to Bucharest was likely.

The strategic position of Czechoslovakia was weakened by the *Anschluss*. Now German forces could threaten from the south, as well as the north and west. German troops moving northeastward from Vienna, up the Morava valley, could attack Czech forces in the rear.

In the late summer of 1938 Germany demanded that Czechoslovakia hand over all territory in which the German-speaking population made up 50 per cent of the inhabitants. This primarily involved the Sudeten lands, which had never been part of Germany. To agree to this would disrupt the economic functioning of Bohemia and Moravia. Czechoslovakia, with an alliance with France and another with the Soviet Union, conditional on French action, prepared to fight. The defences of the country were ready, the army was well equipped, and the mountainous frontier region, abutting Germany, was defensible.

The British prime minister, Neville Chamberlain, fearing that a European war would start in a faraway place, flew to Germany and on 25 September 1938 signed the Munich agreement, along with Germany, Italy and France. Czechoslovakia was pressured into giving up the Sudeten lands and other German-speaking areas. Elizabeth Wiskeman reminded the world of Bismarck's dictum ... 'the master of Bohemia is the master of Europe.'[9] The geopolitical game now took on its own momentum.

After the *Anschluss* and Munich the Soviets feared that Hitler was being turned towards them.[10] That was not Chamberlain's intent but on the map Germany was extending to the east. When Germany disposed of the rump of Czechoslovakia in the spring of 1939, Poland was seen as the next target. At this point Britain and France gave Poland a territorial guarantee. Hitler and Ribbentrop did not take this seriously. Why should they after Munich? And the guarantee was a geopolitical mistake. The Soviet Union saw after Munich that a partition of Poland would be in their interests. By guaranteeing Polish territorial integrity Britain and France, from a Soviet perspective, had removed themselves from any possibility of making a deal that would result in Soviet gains at Polish expense. Britain would have been on firmer ground pressuring Poland to give up territory than she had been with Czechoslovakia. After the First World War Britain had tried to get Poland to accept the Curzon line as the boundary with the Soviet Union and Poland would not give up territory occupied by Ukrainians.

With no territorial cards to play Britain and France sent a low-level delegation to the Soviet Union in the summer of 1939, to seek understandings. Stalin, like Hitler, had a two-front problem. In 1939 Japan and the USSR were fighting in the Far East. If, as now looked certain, Germany was to take Poland then the USSR would get a border with the Reich. It was time to make a deal with Hitler and on 23 August 1939 Molotov and Ribbentrop signed the Non-Aggression Pact that divided Poland and all of East Europe between Germany and the Soviet Union.[11] Further, the USSR was to supply raw materials to Germany, lessening the impact of any wartime blockade.

A few days after the signing of the pact Germany attacked Poland on 1 September 1939. France and Britain declared war with Germany on 3 September, to be quickly followed by Canada, Australia, New Zealand, India and South Africa. Most other countries, including Norway, Sweden, Denmark, the Baltics, Finland and the US, declared neutrality and hoped the war would pass them by.

The Soviet Union attacked Poland from the east on 17 September. By the end of the month the Polish state had ceased to function and its territory was divided between Germany and the Soviet Union. The aggressors were free to expand elsewhere – Stalin into Estonia, Latvia, Lithuania and parts of Finland and Romania. In the spring Germany turned west. On 9 April 1940 the neutral countries of Denmark and Norway were invaded. Denmark was occupied without opposition, hardly a year after it had signed a non-aggression pact with Germany. Norway resisted and did not surrender until 9 June. Meanwhile, in May, neutral Belgium and the neutral Netherlands were attacked along with France. The Netherlands was out of the war in a few days, Belgium surrendered on 28 May, and France sought an armistice on 22 June. British troops had to be lifted off the beaches at Dunkirk earlier in June. Italy entered the war on 10 June 1940, bombed the British naval base at Malta the same day and prepared to attack Egypt and the Suez canal from Libya.

Strategically Germany now dominated Western and Central Europe. At the beginning of 1940 Germany had a small section of the North Sea coast. By the end of June Germany controlled the Atlantic shore of Europe from the Pyrenees to North Cape in Norway. In the early months of 1940 it had been difficult for German submarines to get out into the Atlantic when they had limited entry points between Wilhelmshaven and the North Sea exit of the Kiel canal. By the end of June 1940 the French navy was gone from the Atlantic and the Royal Navy had been outflanked. U-boats were stationed in Norwegian fjords directly facing the Atlantic. From the French ports of Brest, Lorient, La Rochelle and Bordeaux, submarines and their supply vessels could come into the shipping lanes west of the British Isles. Similarly, surface vessels designed to attack merchant shipping could depart from a long sea frontage and spread the reconnaissance forces of the Royal Navy and the Royal Air Force over a much wider area.

Britain lost Europe as a source of imported foodstuffs, iron ore, timber and non-ferrous ores. Now these materials had to be brought to the UK on longer, more costly voyages through waters patrolled by submarines. By July 1940 a German invasion was imminent. But for the *Wehrmacht* to cross the Channel, it had to control the skies above the sea or the Royal Navy would destroy the invasion barges. Germany had few escort vessels when the war started and many of these were sunk in the Norwegian campaign.

In the summer of 1940 the *Luftwaffe* tried to establish air superiority over the Channel and southeastern England as the precondition to operation Sea Lion, the invasion of Britain. The Royal Air Force was put under extreme pressure in the Battle of Britain but retained coherence as a fighting force, capable of intercepting incoming raids. The Royal Air Force did not destroy the *Luftwaffe* but conversely, the *Luftwaffe* failed to cripple the RAF fighter squadrons and establish air superiority. As a result, Sea Lion could not be launched in August or September 1940, and by October, the weather made a cross-Channel invasion nearly impossible. Sea Lion was postponed. On 18 December 1940 Hitler ordered the planning of an attack on the Soviet Union.[12] The codename for the campaign was Barbarossa.

Before Barbarossa, Italian diversions had to be dealt with. In April 1939 Italy had taken Albania. Then in October 1940, without consultation with Germany, Italian forces attacked Greece and were repulsed. In the spring of 1941 Germany sent help, but to reach Greece forces had to go through Yugoslavia and Yugoslavia resisted. The campaign was short and, by the end of April, Yugoslavia and Greece were occupied. Britain sent troops to Greece but they were quickly pushed off the mainland and subsequently Germany took the Aegean island of Crete. From Crete the *Luftwaffe* could attack vessels sailing between Alexandria and Malta and drop mines into the Suez canal. The Balkans campaign was a success but it had consumed time and supplies.

The thaw in East Europe was late in the spring of 1941. On 15 May, the original start date for Barbarossa, the ground was too wet for mechanized warfare and units used in the Balkans were being resupplied and repositioned. Barbarossa, launched in the early hours of the short midsummer night, was highly successful at first. In the north Leningrad was under siege by September. The central group of armies advanced eastward taking Smolensk (5 August) and threatening Moscow. The southern thrust, along the north shore of the Black Sea, captured part of the Ukraine and much of the resources for iron and steel production in the Don region.

Soviet armies were surrounded and destroyed but the USSR did not sue for peace. In November, Stalin, knowing that Japan was to strike at southeast Asia, ordered forces from the Far East into the defence of Moscow. In early December these fresh, experienced units were able to stop the German advance which had already slowed at the end of long supply lines. By November, when the hard frosts arrived, it was obvious that German forces were not equipped for the Russian winter; time and fuel were consumed in keeping men and machines warm.

When Barbarossa was planned the objective was to reach a line running from Archangel, on the Arctic Ocean, to Astrakan on the Caspian Sea.[13] German armies were well short of the line but they had occupied large areas of the Soviet Union and were well positioned for the campaigns of 1942.

There was a strategic debate in the highest German circles on the focus of the Russian campaign. Should the attack be concentrated on Moscow, the command centre of the Soviet totalitarian state, or was it necessary to divide forces to capture resources in the Ukraine (ores and grain) and the oil installations of the Caucasus and the Caspian? The latter strategy was used and failed. There is no certainty that had Moscow been captured the Soviet Union would have collapsed. Many armaments factories were in the east and others were moved to the Volga, the Urals and Siberia as German armies advanced.

Had events gone a little differently there might have been a move towards peace in November 1941. If the German armies had made an earlier start, advanced a little faster, and the winter come a little later, things might have been a bit different. Stalin thought of peace possibilities as Panzer divisions ploughed through the Red Army. Hitler's armaments minister, Todt, and his foreign minister, Ribbentrop, told him to make peace as winter arrived. In 1941, the only other countries fighting against Germany were Britain and her Commonwealth allies, and Britain was struggling to survive the submarine war. If the rate of merchant ship sinkings, in the first half of 1941, had continued throughout the year Britain would have had severe supply problems by November 1941. In June 1941, however, the British codebreakers unravelled the Enigma codes used to direct U-boats in the Atlantic. Now convoys could be diverted away from wolf packs and submarine killers put on patrol in the right place. The British fear of losing the Second World War in the Atlantic receded.

If there had been a peace in 1941 Germany would have been the hegemonic power in Europe. The Soviet Union would still have been vast but shorn of many agricultural and mineral resources in European Russia. Britain would have been peripheral to Europe and cut off from it for trade purposes. The British trading system would have shrunk and with it the economy of the UK. London would have faltered as a financial centre and suffered the fate of Vienna. As far as Britain was concerned the same geopolitical pattern would emerge if there had been a peace after the fall of France in June 1940. Charmley is right in suggesting that continuing the war against Hitler was costly but not fighting would have been ruinous.[14]

In the hypothetical peace of 1941 the United States would have been dominant in the Western Hemisphere but would not have developed a worldwide economic role. Japan, by commercial penetration organized by *Zaibatsu*, would have become economically dominant in southeast Asia at the expense of the former empires of Britain, France, and the Netherlands.

In the light of the above, positive results for Europe and America came from the Japanese attack on the US on 7 December 1941. Germany declared war on 11 December and

Italy followed a few days later. Until December 1941, opinion in the US was strongly against involvement in the war and neutrality acts had been passed to make it difficult to become involved. When Germany attacked Poland the US declared neutrality on 5 September 1939. Trade with belligerents was forbidden and the seas around Europe declared a war zone from which US vessels were excluded. There was some relaxation in November 1939 when belligerents were allowed to trade with the US on a cash and carry basis. Britain and France could now buy materials but the goods could not be carried to British and French ports in US-registered ships. In theory, Germany was free to do the same but the German ports were blockaded by the French and British navies.

The American public, notoriously bad at geography, had no conception of Europe under German control, what that might mean strategically in the Atlantic, and how US exports could be threatened. President Roosevelt did have a strong geostrategic sense and realized that if Britain fell, and Europe came under the control of Germany, US strategic and economic interests would be threatened. But he had to be careful, for political enemies wanted to brand him a warmonger and undermine his support.

After the fall of France, help for Britain increased. Using presidential powers, at the height of the Battle of Britain, Roosevelt transferred 50 First World War destroyers to the Royal Navy and, in exchange, received land for American bases in the Atlantic, which the president had wanted from prewar days.[15] The destroyers-for-bases deal is usually dismissed as a gesture but it was important to the US and the UK. The destroyers needed refitting but their long range and sturdy characteristics made them excellent convoy escort vessels. In return, the US got land in Newfoundland and Bermuda, by gift, and 99-year leases on tracts in the Bahamas, Jamaica, St Lucia, Antigua, Trinidad and British Guiana to construct bases to protect the Atlantic approaches to North America, the Caribbean and northern South America. The Atlantic defences were further strengthened when the US set up bases in Greenland on 10 April 1941 and then took over Iceland from British forces on 7 July 1941.

On 11 March 1941 the Lend Lease Act came into force and made war materials available to Britain on the basis of loan or deferred payment, at a time when Britain was running out of dollars to pay for imports. The USSR benefited from Lend Lease after being attacked by Germany in June 1941.

Britain tried hard to get the US to join the war at a meeting of Churchill and Roosevelt on warships off Argentia, Newfoundland, 9–12 August 1941. The best that could be achieved was the Atlantic Charter which contained the jointly agreed objective of the 'destruction of Nazi tyranny'. In October 1941 the American Neutrality Acts were altered to allow the arming of American merchant ships and their passage into war zones. American vessels could now deliver goods to British ports and relieve the shipping shortage the submarine war had produced.

ROOSEVELT'S GEOSTRATEGIC VIEW

There are numerous interpretations of Roosevelt's intentions regarding US entry into the Second World War. Though we may never know his inner thoughts,[16] we can document Roosevelt's publicly expressed geostrategic views in the months before the US was forced into the war.

On 31 March 1939 in off-the-record remarks made to reporters, after Germany took over the rump of the Czech lands, the president offered the following insight:

> ... the hopes that the world had last September, that the German policy was limited ... to bringing contiguous German people into the Reich and only German people ... those hopes have been dissipated by the events of the last few weeks ... where there was a limit in autumn, there is no limit today ...

The new German policy could mean: 'German domination, not only in all the small nations in Europe but very possibly on other continents'.[17]

These remarks mirror the view of Chamberlain who thought he had bought peace and now knew he had been defrauded.

Early in April 1939, Italy occupied Albania and at a press conference Roosevelt described how Axis expansion would have the effect of curtailing American trade and shipping activity. In the view of Hearnden this concern was an important part of

FDR's decision to confront the dictators.[18] When Britain and France declared war over the German attack on Poland, 3 September 1939, the president delivered a fireside chat in which he reiterated American neutrality but warned that events would have an impact on the US.

In May 1940 as Germany was overrunning France and the neutral countries of Western Europe, the president spelt out, to members of the Senate and the House of Representatives, the danger to America. If Germany took the islands of the Atlantic including Greenland, the Azores, Bermuda and the Cape Verde group, bombers would be within striking distance of the eastern seaboard of the US, the Caribbean and Brazil. Critics may have thought that FDR was scaremongering but documents revealed after the war that Germany did have plans to take, at least, the Canaries and the Azores.[19]

In the fireside chat of 29 December 1940 the country was told that Germany, Japan and Italy had signed a tripartite pact aimed at world control. Germany intended to enslave Europe and use the resources of the region to dominate the world. If Britain went down the Axis would control Europe, Asia, Africa and Australia together with the seas leading to the Western hemisphere.

Some were suggesting a negotiated peace but the president was adamant that no trust could be placed in Nazis pacts or guarantees. Germany claimed that neutral European countries had been occupied to save them from British aggression. Next Germany would occupy South American countries to protect them from the US. A negotiated peace would only be an armistice, leading to a gigantic armaments race and trade war. The fireside chat of 29 December 1940 is known as the Arsenal of Democracy speech for the message was carefully packaged to convey the idea that America would provide the armaments for those fighting fascism but the underlying strategic message was powerful and accurate.[20]

There are important parallels between Churchill and Roosevelt. Both saw that Nazi Germany had geopolitical ambitions far beyond the revision of the Versailles treaty long before their peers. Both had a strong sense of geostrategy and an ability to analyse the importance of territory from a strategic perspective. Both men were branded as warmongers and not allowed fully to develop strategic policies until disaster was close. Churchill became prime minister after the German invasion of neutral Denmark and Norway. Roosevelt could not put the US on a war footing until the Japanese had struck Pearl Harbor, Guam, the Philippines and southeast Asia.

Had Britain entered into a negotiated peace with Germany after the fall of France, as some were prepared to consider, or had the US come to an arrangement with Nazi Germany in 1940 or 1941, the world would have been divided into autarkic power blocs, each seeking to be self-sufficient and limiting world trade.

Roosevelt came to believe that isolationist policies might result in the US being sealed off from overseas contacts. In 1940, in the months before the presidential election, as Germany overran Europe, a large majority of American voters wanted to stay out of the war. Roosevelt saw that voting to avoid war would result in global dominance being conceded to the Axis powers, even if they lacked the ability to invade the US.

Roosevelt ran for a third term to guide the country through the war he knew it could not avoid. He believed that other candidates for the presidency would not confront the danger until the Axis controlled much of the world and had excluded American goods, services and investments.[21]

FIVE

The New Order of 1942

At the beginning of 1942 the world had been divided into warring geopolitical realms. The geopolitical realms were: Europe under German military and economic hegemony; the totalitarian, autarkic, centrally planned Soviet Union; the Maritime World Alliance of the US, the British Commonwealth and the remnants of the Belgian, Danish and Dutch overseas empires; the Pacific Rim dominated by Japan's Greater East Asian Co-Prosperity sphere.

It would be tidy to say, in geopolitical terms, that we have the Maritime World Alliance confronting the dictatorial regimes but that is not the case. The Nazi and Soviet regimes were fighting each other and the USSR was being supported with arms shipments from the UK and the USA. As a result it was likely that the war would end with one of the totalitarian powers controlling many of the assets of Eurasia.

As we have seen, the Soviet Union had the resource base to achieve autarky. This was not the case for Germany but Germany intended to capture the resources of Europe to create a New Order. Milward has defined the New Economic Order in the following way:

> The New Order was an attempt to create within the confines of Europe a *Großraumwirtschaft*, an economy sufficiently autarkic to enable Europe to exist without dependence on other areas either for raw materials or markets. The core of this *Großraumwirtschaft* would be the German manufacturing area in the center of Europe, including Alsace, Lorraine, Bohemia, Moravia, the Austrian territories, and the whole of Silesia. The peripheral areas would be suppliers of foodstuffs and raw materials and purchasers of manufactures.[1]

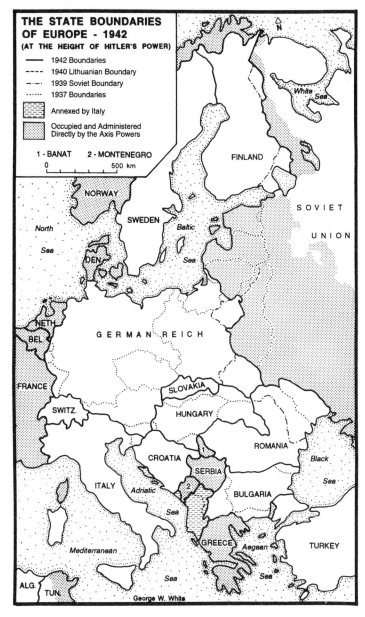

THE STATE BOUNDARIES
OF EUROPE - 1942
(AT THE HEIGHT OF HITLER'S POWER)

——— 1942 Boundaries
- - - - 1940 Lithuanian Boundary
- - · - 1939 Soviet Boundary
· · · · · 1937 Boundaries

Annexed by Italy

Occupied and Administered
Directly by the Axis Powers

1 - BANAT   2 - MONTENEGRO
0   500 km

8 Germany and surrounding territory, 1942.

At the beginning of 1942 Germany had achieved many of her war aims. *Mitteleuropa* was under German control, territory for *Lebensraum* had been taken in Poland and the Ukraine. Controlling more land, raw materials, industrial capacity and lines of communication made it appear that autarky was achievable (illus. 8).

However, the German-dominated economic sphere had been created by conquest and the military campaigns were incomplete. In the east, the Red Army was still a coherent fighting force. In the west the Royal Navy and the Royal Air Force blockaded the ports of Europe and reduced imports to a fraction of prewar levels. Sealed off from many Soviet raw materials coming from the east and imports entering via West European ports, Germany now had to attain autarky within the European economic area it controlled.

The German Four-Year Plan, adopted in 1936, had a goal of self-sufficiency. However, conservation, substitutions and synthetic products could only go part way to replacing lost imports. Most of the synthesized products needed more energy to make them than it took to transport the natural product to Germany. German coalfields were rich, but in wartime they could not meet all of the increasing demand.

The supply problems were understood by military planners in Germany before the Second World War. The *Wehrmacht* knew it did not have the raw materials and industrial capacity to fight a long war. Studies had shown that only '44.4 per cent of the necessary requirement of imported foodstuffs and 33 per cent of the requirement of imported raw materials could be regarded as relatively secure!'[2] If Germany was to create autarky it would be necessary to utilize the raw materials, agricultural output, and industrial capacity of occupied territory in a sustainable manner.

GERMAN ECONOMIC REGIONS

The economic regions that Germany controlled in 1942 were:
1. Axis-dominated Central Europe: Sweden to Sicily
2. German-dominated East Europe: The Middle Tier

3. Occupied lands in the Soviet Union

4. Occupied Western Europe

1. Axis-dominated Central Europe

This included Sweden, Germany, Austria (since 1938 in union with Germany), Switzerland and Italy. Prior to the Second World War, Germany had the strongest economy in Europe with steel production (24 million metric tons) nearly twice that of the UK (13 million metric tons) and larger than the Soviet Union (18 million metric tons). Germany had well-developed non-ferrous metallurgical industries including aluminium, copper, zinc and lead smelting. Germany possessed a technologically advanced manufacturing sector including motor vehicles, aircraft, electronics, chemicals and armaments. By the use of cartels, cross-border investments and bi-lateral trade agreements Germany had strong linkages with the economies of Central and Eastern Europe. Germany produced and exported a surplus of coal. It had to import iron ore, non-ferrous minerals, rubber and, above all, oil.

Sweden, Switzerland and Austria were well integrated with the economy of Germany. Sweden exported iron ore to Germany and supplied special steels, precision equipment and machinery. Switzerland and Austria had high-quality metallurgical industries that exported to Germany, and Switzerland, like Sweden, manufactured precision equipment and some armaments. As neutrals the war-related industries of Sweden and Switzerland were free of allied bombing.

Italy had metallurgical, chemical, shipbuilding, vehicle and aircraft industries. The country lacked self-sufficiency in all major raw materials including coal, oil and iron ore. Prewar Italy had traded extensively by sea. In 1942 the country was under blockade and even coastal shipping was disrupted. The loss of seaborne imports meant that Germany had to provide more industrial inputs. The supplies never came in sufficient quantities and Italian industry did not produce to its full potential.

Beyond the core of the Axis region were North Africa, Spain and Finland. The Italian colonies in Tripolitanea and Cyrenica exported little of value. (The oil was not exploited until after the Second World War.) Spain, under a fascist government, was recovering from a civil war (1936–9). Hitler wanted Spain in the war as a platform to attack Gibraltar. Germany could not guarantee the supplies of oil and grain Franco needed, while the US did provide credits to allow Spain to buy commodities, and the Royal Navy issued the *navicerts* to let the materials reach Spanish ports.[3] Spain stayed out of the war but ore exports to Germany grew rapidly, including wolfram, the starting point for tungsten, the steel hardener.

A major source of nickel, for Germany, was in Kolosjokki in northern Finland.[4] Finland having been invaded by the USSR in 1939 signed a peace early in 1940 but re-entered the war at the onset of Barbarossa, hoping to regain territory.

2. German-dominated East Europe

Prewar Germany was the major trading partner of all the countries of East Europe – Poland, Czechoslovakia, Hungary, Romania, Bulgaria, Yugoslavia and Greece. Czechoslovakia (steel output 2.3 million metric tons) had industrial capacity in textiles, glass, chemicals, vehicles and armaments, along with resources like coal (17 million metric tons of hard coal produced in 1937), iron, graphite, copper and lead. Output increased in the Czech lands after it became a protectorate of the Reich (Slovakia was nominally autonomous). Later in the war raw material shortages curtailed industrial output,[5] but steel output was 2.5 million metric tons in 1944.

Germany occupied western Poland so rapidly in September 1939 that much industrial capacity – particularly the coal mines and heavy industry of Silesia – was taken intact. In Polish Silesia, Germany acquired coal, lead and zinc supplies together with steel-making capacity. Prior to partition Poland produced 1.4 million metric tons of steel in 1938.

Bulgaria, Hungary and Romania joined the Axis cause in 1941 but linked with Germany economically long before then. Hungary had major deposits of bauxite and some oil. Romania produced ores of iron, copper, lead and zinc and was the largest oil producer in Europe. In 1938 Romanian wells produced

6.6 million metric tons of oil. The USSR output was 28 million metric tons and the US produced 170 million metric tons.

Hungary manufactured some machinery and electrical goods but overall the industrial capacity of southeast Europe was limited. The same was true of Yugoslavia and Greece, invaded in the spring of 1941. Yugoslavia had ores of chrome, zinc, manganese, lead and copper which Germany continued to import during the war.

Because Germany enjoyed strong economic connections with the countries of Central and East Europe before the war she was able to integrate them into the war economy of the Reich. In 1942 the concept of a German-dominated *Mitteleuropa*, in its literal sense of middle Europe, was reality. Sweden and Switzerland escaped occupation but their economies were largely dependent upon interaction with Germany.

However, when all the gains in manufacturing capacity and raw material output in *Mitteleuropa* were added up it was clear that Germany had not established the foundation for autarky. In the east oil and ores had to be taken from the Soviet Union. In the west the manufacturing capacity and specialized agriculture had to be integrated into the economy of the Reich if Germany were to create dominance in a greater European economic region and win the war.

3. Occupied lands in the Soviet Union

Hitler had several objectives when he ordered that Russia be crushed 'in a rapid campaign'.[6] He wished to complete a drive to the east that would make Germany master of Eurasia. If the Soviet Union had been knocked off the geopolitical board then Japan would have had no mainland power at her back and would have been free to expand in the Pacific, putting pressure on the US. Under pressure the US would have been able to give less aid to Britain and the UK would have been more likely to make peace.[7]

The resource objectives were to acquire agricultural land, ores and oil in Soviet territory. The cities of Leningrad and Moscow were to be reduced to rubble. The Slav inhabitants of the conquered region were to be driven out, killed off or starved to death.

From a German perspective a major problem was that one could penetrate a long way into Soviet territory and not encounter much mineral wealth other than the oil shales of Estonia. Moscow, Leningrad, Smolensk and Kiev were large manufacturing centres, at the core of the most densely populated part of the Soviet Union, but the raw materials for the industries in the cities were brought in from the east.

The Ukraine, with its rich black earth (loess) had great agricultural potential and in the Don Basin there were major deposits of coal and high-grade iron ore. Beyond the Don Valley, and the transportation centre of Rostov, lay the Volga, the great navigable river that linked the region lying between Moscow and the Urals to the Caspian Sea. Southeast of Rostov, at a distance of nearly 500 miles, were the Caucasus mountains. On the north side of the upland were the oilfields at Grosny and Maikop. Beside the Caspian, around Baku, were larger oilfields. In the view of Hitler and others in the German high command, capture of the oilfields was essential to sustain the German war effort. In 1942 Germany did take oil from the Grosny area but the amounts were not large.

The main problem for the *Wehrmacht* in attacking the Soviet Union was distance. It was 800 miles from Königsberg (Kaliningrad) in East Prussia to Leningrad, approximately 1,000 miles from Warsaw to Moscow, and over 1,200 miles from Krakow to Rostov. Across these distances armies had to be moved and supplied, quickly, if Red Army resistance was to be crushed before the winter arrived. At first all went well. By November 1941 German forces occupied territory that, prewar, had contained 40 per cent of the Soviet population, 71 per cent of the iron ore mined, 63 per cent of coal output, 58 per cent of the crude steel production and 42 per cent of the prewar electricity-generating capacity. Soviet manufacturing output and arms production plummeted. But Soviet losses were not Germany's gain. The USSR practised 'a strategy of denial'.[8] Key industrial plants were moved east or destroyed. Harrison estimates that one-eighth of all Soviet industrial assets were relocated in the Second World War.[9] Engineering plants, aircraft factories, the Kharkov T34 tank assembly unit and whole iron and steel works were removed to the east. The five-year plans had created industrial infrastructure in the Volga, Urals, Kuznetsk, and Vladivostock regions. Plants and skilled labour could be relocated to the new or expanded industrial regions. Nearly half of the evacuated factories were moved to the Urals.[10] In spite of removals, production was dramatically down. In the first half of 1942 coal production was at one-third the level of the previous year. Electricity generation was at 50 per cent and steel output was at 40 per cent.[11]

Soviet troops in retreat systematically destroyed locomotive sheds, watering stations and the technical apparatus of the rail system.[12] One result was a transportation disaster for Germany in November 1941. The front was not moving quickly enough to gain the Archangel–Astrakhan (A-A) line – the target which the Germans believed would render the Soviet Union incapable of continuing the war – and winter was arriving. At Leningrad, the mean monthly temperature for November is below freezing. The rapid campaign had not been sufficiently rapid to bring victory before the long, cold continental winter that came every year to the Soviet Union set in. The *Wehrmacht* was not equipped for a war in the Russian winter and lacked enough heavy clothing and anti-freeze for vehicles and other equipment.

In early December, in front of Moscow, the Red Army, reinforced by units from the Far East, counter-attacked and drove German forces back. The *Wehrmacht* dug in to survive in an environment that freezes, and stays below freezing, from December through March. The Ukraine is south of Moscow but the winter is still harsh. The Dneister, Dnieper and Don rivers freeze. The northeast wind – the *buran* – blows across the Ukraine from Siberia pushing wind chill indexes below zero. Men die of exposure in such conditions as was to happen at Stalingrad, on the Volga, in the winter of 1942–3.

Flying over the Ukraine in January 1942, Speer reported:

On large farms we saw the burned sheds and barns. To keep our direction, we flew along the railroad line. Scarcely a train could be seen; the stations were burnt out, the round-houses destroyed. Roads were rare, and they too were empty of vehicles. The great stretches of land we passed over were

frightening in their deathly silence ... only gusts of snow
broke the monotony of the landscape ... [13]

Before Christmas 1941 Goebbels, the propaganda chief, was
forced to make a public appeal to German civilians to give
overcoats, underwear, lined boots, earmuffs and gloves to be
sent to the Russian front.[14] Many in Germany now understood that the campaign in the east was in great trouble,
although there would be more advances in the spring and
summer of 1942.

The reasons for the inability of the rapid campaign to bring
victory by Christmas were numerous. The failure to create a
decisive battle in front of Moscow, as a result of pursuing too
many objectives, is high on the lists of most commentators.
Postwar analysis indicates that the whole Soviet economic
system was close to collapse in 1941–2.[15] Had Moscow, at the
heart of the transportation and administrative system, been
captured in late 1941, it would have been difficult to organize
the Soviet war effort and Moscow had the largest manufacturing base of any Soviet city.

The logistic problems of operating in Soviet space were
underestimated as was the quantity of Soviet defence assets. At
the beginning of the Second World War there was a widely
held opinion that the Red Army had obsolete equipment,
lacked good leadership and would collapse quickly against
Panzer divisions supported by the *Luftwaffe*.[16] There were
good reasons for this view. In 1937 Stalin purged the Red Army
of senior officers, perceived to be politically suspect, and produced a shortage of commanders with wartime experience.
The Red Army had much old equipment and the war the
Soviets started against Finland, on 30 November 1939,
resulted in high casualties. Although Finland was forced to sign
a peace, on 12 March 1940, the winter war substantiated the
idea that the Red Army was poorly equipped and badly led.

One prewar commentator saw the picture differently.
Basseches pointed out that the USSR had 17–18 million persons with military training. The armaments industry was not
dependent upon imported parts or raw materials. A significant
proportion of the armament factories was in the Urals, or the

Kuznetsk Basin in Siberia, beyond the range of air strikes. And the new equipment coming out of the factories, including the T34 tank, was of high quality. There would be no shortage of men, machines and ammunition if the Soviet Union went to war. We can add that there was no shortage of Soviet space in which to employ the strategy of denial and to disperse strategic industries away from the front.[17]

In spite of the logistical problems, if the campaign against the Soviet Union had been conducted wholly as a military campaign, the *Wehrmacht* would have had a much better chance of winning. But Hitler had resource objectives and his geopolitical vision was linked to racial views. In Hitler's mind *Lebensraum* was a racial as well as a spatial concept. The folk who were to occupy *Lebensraum* in the east were to be of Nordic blood; the Slavs were to be driven out. Unlike German policy-makers in the First World War who wanted to break the Russian hold on non-Russian people, Hitler treated all Slavs as one vast group of *Untermenschen*. When German armies reached the Ukraine they entered a land where collectivized agriculture had been imposed with executions, deportations and starvation. Many Ukrainians were happy to be rid of the Soviet system. Instead of exploiting the resentments of non-Russian peoples, a policy of destruction, exploitation and neglect was followed which resulted in powerful partisan groups operating behind German lines. Michael Burleigh has documented the manner in which German academics, studying the peoples of East Europe, followed the party line and depicted Slavs as inferior to Germans, making it difficult to think of cooperation with Ukrainians.[18]

It was not just the political possibilities that were ignored. Germany had excellent climatologists including Köppen who in the 1930s was publishing the multi-volume *Handbuch der Klimatologie*. But there is little evidence that climatologists helped plan the timetable of Barbarossa. An exhaustive study of the planning of the campaign shows that in the organizational phase many of the problems were discussed. For example 'a military-geographical study of European Russia' of August 1940 set out the importance of Leningrad and Moscow as major manufacturing centres but pointed out that there were industrial regions to the east and it could not be assumed that the fall of Leningrad and Moscow would mean the end of the war. The military geographers stressed the climate problem and the issue of distance.[19]

In the end, advice that stressed difficulties was largely ignored. The objective was more important than the objections. Other military machines made the same mistake. Late in the war British paratroopers were used to take a bridge too far – the Rhine bridge at Arnhem. Before the operation, intelligence revealed, from oblique air photos, that there was a German tank force within striking distance of the bridge. Lightly armed paratroopers cannot combat tanks and the operation should have been called off. But the commanders had a momentum of their own, the troops were dropped, the operation failed, losses were heavy.[20]

The totalitarian regimes of Nazi Germany and the Soviet Union shared one objective in the battles fought between them – they wanted to destroy the landscape. As the Red Army retreated, farms, factories and transportation equipment were wrecked or removed. On taking territory German special forces often reduced towns to rubble and killed local inhabitants. Later, when the *Wehrmacht* retreated, it destroyed facilities that had been repaired and brought back into use.

The main economic objective of Barbarossa was to acquire grains, coal, metal ores and oil from conquered lands. In the initial plan there was little interest in utilizing Soviet manufacturing capacity. How local populations were to be utilized was not adequately considered. There was the overall objective of settling Nordics in newly acquired *Lebensraum* but that would take years to produce agricultural surpluses. In the meantime who was going to grow the grain and dig the coal and ores Germany wanted? As a German officer put it – if you kill off or starve all the Ukrainians 'who will produce economic assets here?'[21] And the army did use practical policies to restart facilities that could be used to repair tanks and reopened factories that made carts.

Overall only a few hundred thousand tons of grain per year were sent back from the Ukraine to Germany during the Occupation. The area in cultivation was much less than in prewar years and yields were lower. On the mineral resources front, by the end of 1942, the Donets coalfield was producing 10,000 tons a day, although many mines were not back in production. At Nikopol, manganese production was restarted by the end of 1941 and by 1943 more manganese was being produced than before the war. Little oil was extracted from the north Caucasus. By the summer of 1942 about a fifth of the prewar electricity-generating capacity had been restored and in June the following year the huge Dneprostroi hydroelectric system was brought back into operation. The Krivoy Rog iron ore mines were producing at a low level by the end of 1942 and early in 1943 some iron and steel works, such as those at Stalino and Zaporozh'ye, were in production. Some agricultural equipment was produced as Germany became more interested in manufacturing capacity as the Occupation progressed.[22]

Dallin estimates that Germany extracted from the east only about one-seventh of the produce and products that were taken out of France.[23] Overall, Barbarossa was a military and economic failure. The resources that would have come to Germany from the Soviet Union, under the commercial treaties associated with the 1939 pact, were lost and the costly campaign did not replace them, even in the short run.

4. Occupied Western Europe

Before the end of 1941 German forces in the east were suffering chronic shortages of fuel and equipment. German warfare had not been fully mechanized. Artillery pieces, ammunition carts and many supply trucks were horse-drawn. Infantry frequently marched and were left behind by the tanks as there was not enough transport. Part of the transportation problem was due to the destruction of the rail system but overall the army did not have the trucks and half-tracks to adopt fully mechanized warfare.

Western Europe had the manufacturing capacity to fill many German equipment needs if Germany harnessed industries to the war machine. However, the big picture, as set out at the beginning of this chapter, saw Germany as the manufacturing heart of Europe and outer regions as suppliers of resources. In general, German geopolitics with emphasis on territory,

Lebensraum, and mineral resources did not give sufficient weight to the importance of manufacturing capacity in occupied lands.

In the discussion at the Royal Geographical Society in January 1904, at the end of Mackinder's Pivot paper, L. S. Amery made the point that to win wars in the future you would have to employ science, technology and more industrial capacity than your rivals. On 2 September 1939, on the eve of the war, *The Economist* suggested that the side which was most successful in harnessing its industrial power to the forces on the battlefield would win.

Hitler could never do the industrial capacity sums and by the time people like Speer took charge of such matters it was too late. Hitler failed to understand that the US could produce enough armaments to fight wars in the Pacific and Atlantic simultaneously and provide the Red Army with trucks and jeeps. In 1914 the German chancellor wanted to integrate Europe economically, with Germany as the dominant power. The Third Reich was to employ a *Blitzkrieg* economic policy in 1940, 1941 and much of 1942, with the aim of stripping men, material and machines out of the manufacturing sector of Western Europe.

During the war the economies of Western Europe shrank. International trade declined. Agricultural production decreased and industrial output about halved. Shorn of imported inputs, industry and agriculture could not produce at prewar levels. In theory, if Germany wanted a self-sufficient Europe, the exclusion of imports was to be welcomed but wartime experience showed that it was impossible for the region to function effectively, if cut off from overseas imports (illus. 9).

The problems quickly became apparent in Denmark, a country that suffered little damage in the German invasion. Denmark specialized in the production of livestock and livestock products including ham, beef, poultry, eggs and dairy goods. About a third of the economically active population worked in farming and the land was cultivated intensively to produce many crops that were fed to animals. The system required heavy inputs of fertilizer – natural and artificial – together with the use of cheap, imported feedstuffs from North America. In wartime the application of artificial fertilizers

9 Cartoon of 19 May 1941 by Dr Seuss. University of California, San Diego, Mandeville Special Collections Library (Dr. Seuss Collection).

declined, crop yields dropped and the loss of imported grains made the livestock feed problem worse. Prewar Britain had been the major market for Danish exports and perhaps the exports could be redirected overland to markets in German industrial towns. However, production declined so much that there was little to export. In 1938 Denmark imported 667,000 metric tons of grain; in 1941 the import figure was 5,000 metric tons; in 1938 78 million score of eggs were exported; in 1942 5 million score of eggs were exported; in 1938 meat exports were 214,000 metric tons and in 1942 meat exports were down to 38,000 metric tons.[24]

Table 1 Crop areas in selected countries.

		Hectares in wheat	Hectares in potatoes
Austria	1938	250,000	215,000
	1946	200,000	156,000
Belgium	1938	174,000	147,000
	1946	138,000	79,000
Czechoslovakia	1938	897,000	763,000
	1946	900,000	640,000
Denmark	1938	132,000	79,000
	1946	90,000	103,000
France	1938	5,050,000	1,425,000
	1946	4,131,000	852,000
Germany	1938	2,094,000	2,893,000
	1944	1,781,000	2,764,000
Netherlands	1938	126,000	130,000
	1946	122,000	203,000
Norway	1938	35,000	54,000
	1946	38,000	62,000
UK	1938	778,000	247,000
	1946	834,000	498,000

Notes
1. Harvests are variable.
2. Countries suffered different impacts from the war and some countries recovered more quickly than others.
3. In the above list, wheat hectares are down, with the exception of the UK and Norway. Hectares in wheat and potatoes went up in the Second World War in Norway and were higher during the war than in 1946. Norway was a food importer pre-war. When imports were cut off during the war, much marginal land was brought into cultivation. Marginal land can be defined as agricultural land on which crop yields are insufficient to justify the costs of cultivation when competing agricultural areas can produce crops more cheaply. During the war, Norway was cut off from imports and land was converted from pasture to arable.

Source: B. R. Mitchell, *International Historical Statistics: Europe, 1750–1993* (New York, 1998), 4th edn.

Prior to the Second World War Germany was the largest trading partner of the Netherlands, a country with advanced technological industries and efficient agriculture. No West European country was to suffer as badly as the Netherlands before the war was over. In May 1940 the Netherlands was bombed and occupied in a few days. The merchant marine, at sea, diverted to allied ports, the government moved to London, to join the Dutch overseas empire to the allied cause, and the multinational corporations, like Royal Dutch Shell, moved financial assets to the Dutch West Indies, putting those territories on the road to becoming offshore financial centres.

In Amsterdam industries like diamond cutting that depended upon imported raw materials began to run down. Deprived of inputs like feedstuffs and fertilizers the intensive farming system faltered.[25] In 1940–41, the first year of occupation, Germany imported 49 million metric tons of meat and 28 million metric tons of butter from the Netherlands. By 1941–2 only 27 million metric tons of meat and 3 million metric tons of butter reached Germany.[26] As farmers reverted to basic crops exports of grains and potatoes to Germany increased.

France had a more traditional farming system with strong elements of self-sufficiency. French farmers did not use large quantities of artificial fertilizer, imported feedstuffs, or mechanized equipment like tractors. Perhaps the system would not be greatly impacted by war. However, as in the First World War, French farm output fell rapidly. The traditional farm economy relied upon high labour inputs and 35 per cent of the French workforce was in farming. As conscription and forced labour removed workers from the land, and horses were requisitioned for military purposes, the area under crops shrank, yields per hectare declined and livestock herds produced less meat and milk. German agriculture, even with forced labour, underwent similar trends (see Tables 1, 2).

Vineyards and olive groves declined little in area but the output of wine in France and olive oil in Italy fell sharply as labour was withdrawn from fields and processing plants.

Food shortages were common in the occupied territories. By the end of the war the Dutch population was starving and reduced to eating bulbs, which were reported to be tasty when fried. Most Europeans got used to eating less animal protein and more bread and potatoes as an age-old law reasserted itself: when food is scarce, crops are grown for direct human consumption, and the luxury of feeding grains to livestock, which consume ten pounds of feed to add a pound in weight, is greatly reduced. The livestock herds, in many parts of Europe, did not disappear: there was plenty of grazing on formerly cultivated land where they could put on weight slowly and produce low outputs of milk. The feeding of grains to animals was greatly reduced and large-scale pig production, which consumed many feedstuffs, was run down and the animals slaughtered.

From 1914 until 1948, farming in Europe went from one crisis to another. The First World War caused production declines, the postwar era did not bring stability, and in the Great Depression farm prices collapsed and export markets, for many products, disappeared.[27] The Second World War restored demand for foodstuffs but through lack of labour and other inputs the demand could not be supplied. Most civilians at one time or another went short of food in the Second World War and many suffered alarming losses of body weight.[28]

The impact of these forces on the creation of the EEC Common Agricultural Policy (the CAP) will always be debated. But a policy that gave generous guaranteed prices to overproduce grain, livestock, dairy products, wine and vegetable oils could be sold to populations that remembered food shortages and embraced by farmers who understood that guaranteed markets meant higher prices. Today, there are high food prices in the EU and, for many products, subsidized self-sufficiency or surplus.

Prior to the Second World War Germany was not the major trading partner of the countries of Western Europe, as she was in Eastern Europe. It would be more difficult to produce economic integration in the West than in the East. The major trade partner of Norway and Denmark was Britain. Belgium's leading trade partner was France who, in turn, exchanged more goods with Algeria than any other country. Trade between France and Germany was tiny. The Netherlands, on the basis of transit trade on the Rhine, did more trade with Germany than any other country. Now sea commerce to the Rhine and

Germany was lost, as was Germany's trade with Britain, her single largest trading partner. Germany was only eighth on the UK's list of trading partners by value.

Britain had been the major supplier of coal to France, Norway, Denmark, Sweden and Finland and an important provider to the Netherlands and Italy. If key industries in Western Europe were to operate at capacity, Germany would have to supply more coal at a time when demand for fuel was rising rapidly in German manufacturing regions. The needed coal never arrived from Germany to replace imports from Britain and the West European manufacturing sector contracted.

West European steel industries, with the exception of Luxembourg, produced less metal during the war than they did before the war. Ore-rich Luxembourg was well integrated with coal-rich Germany and steel production rose from 1.4 million metric tons in 1938 to 2.1 million metric tons in 1943. In France and Belgium output declined in the same period and coal shortages were a factor in output losses.

In 1939 Western Europe produced little oil. The fuel was imported from the Persian Gulf, the Dutch East Indies, the Caribbean and the US. Once Europe was under blockade oil imports ceased. Western Europe was short of oil and coal. Fuel for domestic heating, transportation and manufacturing was always scarce.

France had the largest manufacturing sector in Western Europe and France's major prewar source of imports was the US. A major component of the imports was industrial equipment. After June 1940 French industry could look forward to shortages of fuels, spare parts and new equipment. Table 7 shows that industrial production fell during the war by approximately 60 per cent – it took more than shortages of spare parts and energy to achieve that! Industries conserve and improvise to prevent such drastic falls in output.

The major additional cause of industrial contraction in Western Europe was *Blitzkrieg* economics. The term *Blitzkrieg* literally means lightning war. *Blitzkrieg* was a campaigning technique and an economic policy. Under the *Blitzkrieg* economic concept, occupied territory would produce raw materials, fuels, foodstuffs, labour (much of it forced) and industrial equipment.[29]

Table 2 Total national production of wheat and potatoes in metric tons.

		Wheat	Potatoes
Austria	1938	441,000	3,257,000
	1946	228,000	1,533,000
Belgium	1938	548,000	3,258,000
	1946	366,000	1,477,000
Czechoslovakia	1938	1,764,000	7,358,000
	1946	1,320,000	9,159,000
Denmark	1938	461,000	1,433,000
	1946	298,000	1,810,000
France	1938	9,800,000	17,310,000
	1946	6,760,000	9,880,000
Germany	1938	6,250,000	55,983,000
	1944	3,808,000	41,240,000
Netherlands	1938	434,000	2,843,000
	1946	359,000	4,245,000
Norway	1938	72,000	938,000
	1946	80,000	1,204,000
UK	1938	1,990,000	4,475,000
	1944	3,184,000	8,155,000

Source: Mitchell (1998).

Blitzkrieg economics and the New Economic Order of Nazi propaganda were incompatible. The maximum economic strength would result from Norway, Denmark, the Netherlands, Belgium and France producing efficiently to support the German war effort. *Blitzkrieg* economic policy, in which raw materials, machinery and manpower were stripped out of the occupied territories and removed to Germany, disrupted the economies of Western Europe. France did not produce the quantity of manufactured goods of which she was capable. Denmark and the Netherlands could not export the quantities of meat and dairy produce that the German war effort needed.

The economies of Western Europe suffered on two fronts.

They lost the imported inputs that came from the maritime world and assets were stripped out of countries to provide resources to industries in Germany.

Milward shows that when Germany realized she was in for a long war, in January 1942, economic policy was altered. There was more interest in 'a continuing contribution from occupied territories'.[30] The German Ministry of War Production tried to stop the plundering and promote integration, although this did not entirely stop the removal of skilled workers to Germany.

When Speer became armaments minister, in 1942, he began to talk about European economic integration and had meetings with the French minister of industrial production (Bichelonne) in Berlin in September 1943 but by then it was too late – Germany was losing the war and any improved French contribution was tiny compared with the output of the US. But what if the French motor industry had been fully harnessed to German needs in 1940 and 1941? Would there have been a different result in the East?

Blitzkrieg economics had impacts on West European trade patterns. Overall, cross-border trade was diminished but inevitably the occupied territories did a large proportion of their trade with Germany and this reversed an inter-war trend. In the period 1928–38, German trade was increasing with southeast Europe, Egypt, Turkey, the Near East, Latin America and north Europe. German trade with Western Europe, Britain and the US was declining in percentage terms.[31] Germany directed trade using bilateral trade agreements towards southeast Europe, the Middle East and Latin America: regions where Germany was building political influence. By 1942 trade links with Latin America and the Middle East, other than Turkey, were cut. Turkey remained a major source of chrome for German armaments until 1944.

In Western Europe the value of international trade declined when 1938 is compared with 1943. In some cases the loss of international trade was spectacular. In 1938, the Netherlands imported 1,460 million Dutch gilders worth of goods. In 1943 imports were valued at 482 million gilders. Exports in 1938 were worth 1,079 million gilders. By 1943 exports amounted to 617 million gilders.

In every West European case, the value of imports declined more precipitously than exports. In wartime there were few goods to import. Exports went predominantly to Germany. At first sight all the conquered countries had favourable trade balances with Germany. Every country exported more to Germany than it received in imports. However, each defeated country was charged for the costs of the German army occupying it. The occupation charges paid for the goods Germany imported from Western Europe.

France displayed an exceptional trade pattern during the Occupation. Overall the international trade of France declined between 1938 and 1943 but the value of exports was greater in 1943 than 1938.[32] Only France achieved such an increase. Of the 35 million francs worth of exports France produced in 1943, 29 million went to Germany. In 1938, France had exported 1.8 million francs worth of goods to Germany! Many sectors of the French economy discovered new markets in wartime and they did not disappear when hostilities ceased. As Milward tells us, by 1943 France had become 'the most important supplier of raw materials, foodstuffs, and manufactured goods to the German economy'.[33] The pattern of West European trade that developed after the Second World War was emerging.

From a geopolitical perspective the Vichy policy towards Germany can be defended as realistic. By the end of June 1940 for France 'the war was over, and Germany had won'.[34] France could come to terms with this if 'she practiced a policy of … collaboration with Germany and Italy and integrated herself … in a reorganized continental Europe'.[35]

The idea of an integrated Europe was not a new policy for it is exactly what Briand had been promoting in the 1920s and early 1930s (chapter 3). The idea had wide circulation in French politics between the wars. During the war the economies of France and Germany became interlinked in a way that had not been so in peacetime. Many large French businesses were able to gain contracts to supply Germany with their products. The war provided the opportunity to start the economic integration that Briand's prewar political initiatives had envisaged. Hitler wanted hegemony, not integration, but there were influential Germans, like Speer, who wanted to create a European union.

During the war French government became more bureaucratized and gained control of economic matters.[36] This did not change after the war as planning, under Monnet, became the basis of economic recovery. De Gaulle would come to power for a short time at the end of the war and propose unsuccessfully a harsh geopolitical peace for Germany. French bureaucrats and businessmen who had seen the possibilities of economic cooperation were able, after a few years, to get the policies they wanted, starting with the Coal and Steel Community in 1951. Before collaboration could become Community cooperation Laval had to be taken out and shot and there had to be summary executions of supposed collaborators and public humiliations of ordinary folk who had day-to-day contact with German troops. Few businessmen and bureaucrats suffered in the indignant denial of Vichy and the violence was quite successful in camouflaging the past. In reality, there had been a line of development that ran from Briand's united Europe, through the experience of Vichy and occupied France, to the Coal and Steel Community and beyond.

THE MARITIME WORLD

In 1942 the maritime world consisted of the British Commonwealth, the United States, Latin America and the overseas interests of the Netherlands, Norway, Denmark and Belgium. Britain and the US could no longer trade in the Far East and mainland Europe (other than the Iberian peninsula) but their ability to manufacture and interact with each other was substantial.

Britain had lost many trading partners in Europe but the situation was not as bad as it appeared. In 1938 Britain's major trading partners were the US, Australia, Canada, South Africa, India, Argentina, New Zealand, Germany, the Netherlands and France. The UK ran an adverse trade balance with every country on the list but narrowed the foreign exchange gap by providing shipping, banking, insurance services and collecting dividends on overseas investments. For example, Britain imported twice as much by value as she exported to Argentina in 1938. But many ranches on the Pampas were British owned, as were railroads, utilities, meat packing plants and the banks in Buenos Aires that financed the meat and grain trade. The dividends from overseas investments, together with profits from financial services and shipping, provided the 'invisible exports' that helped reduce trade imbalances.

The closing of the ports of Europe to overseas trade did not deprive Britain of her top seven trading partners and, as the links with the US, the Commonwealth and Latin America were of long standing, it was possible to increase imports from these sources. If Germany had the capacity to import more from Eastern Europe, Britain had a greater ability to increase imports from overseas sources.

The food and raw material resources of the Commonwealth were large. Canada (wheat and meat), Australia (wheat, mutton, wool and fruit), New Zealand (mutton, wool, butter) and South Africa (fruit) were established exporters of agricultural commodities to Britain. The Caribbean colonies provided sugar, bananas and citrus. West Africa was a source of cocoa, palm oil (for making margarine) and timber. The Indian empire produced tea and raw cotton, while southeast Asia, before being overrun by Japan, exported rice, timber, tin and rubber to Britain.

Beyond the formal British empire was an informal empire where British investments had shaped economies. Argentina and Uruguay were large exporters of grains, beef, mutton and meat products to Britain.

The US was Britain's largest trading partner before the war, and imports of foodstuffs could be increased from that source if US dollars were available. Products from within the sterling area (the area in which the British pound was the major currency of trade) could be paid for in pounds, and supplying countries accumulated large credits in London. Until Lend-Lease arrived in April 1941, finding dollars on demand was a problem, and the British government pressured UK companies to sell US investments to get dollars. The US economy had much unused capacity and expanded rapidly during the war.

The British Empire was a major source of raw materials and

fuel. Canada produced non-ferrous metals, South Africa gold and diamonds, copper came from Northern Rhodesia (Zambia), Australia mined lead, copper, gold, silver, tin and zinc. Via the Anglo-Iranian Oil Company (a forerunner of BP), the British government had a large, direct investment in Middle Eastern oil.

Utilizing the US, Commonwealth countries and the former Dutch and Belgium colonies, Britain had no shortage of sources of food and raw materials, provided the products could be shipped to British ports. Early in the war, shipping was not a problem. Britain had a large merchant marine and additional vessels could be chartered from the fleets that fled European ports in the spring of 1940. However, after the fall of Norway and France, German submarines and aircraft could operate all along the Atlantic coast from Narvik to Bordeaux, and shipping losses mounted.

When the war started in September 1939, Germany had approximately 55 submarines. This fleet was rapidly built up, and the tonnage of allied shipping lost in the North Atlantic was massive. Between June and December 1940, after Germany got control of the Atlantic coast of Europe, just under 3 million tons of merchant ships were sunk by German U-boats, surface raiders and aircraft. In 1941 nearly 900 merchant vessels were lost, totalling 3.3 million tons of shipping. In 1942, as transatlantic crossings increased, 7.8 million tons of shipping were lost, of which 6.3 million tons were sunk by U-boats. Losses were high in early 1943 until increased U-boat sinkings drove the wolf packs from the Atlantic.

For a great part of the war, the UK suffered scarcities and shortages. The British government, aware of the experience of the First World War, when Britain had suffered supply shortages as a result of submarine warfare, put the economy of the UK on a war footing early. In 1938 Britain began to stockpile strategic materials. In 1939 a Ministry of Supply was set up to coordinate arms production. In the same year, the Agricultural Development Act gave subsidies to farmers who ploughed up grazing land to grow arable crops. Conscription was introduced in May 1939 for men aged 20 and 21. In September, with the outbreak of war, conscription was applied to all men in the age bracket 18–41. Essential workers in war-related occupations were exempted (in contrast with Germany).

In 1940 labour was being allocated by the government to strategic industries and in 1941 skilled labour was required to move into essential war industries. Few policy-makers in Britain thought the war would be short and the economy was put on a total war footing long before Germany did the same.

The rationing of basic foods was introduced early in the war. Quickly it became impossible to buy a new car and by 1942 there was no petrol ration for existing private cars except to persons employed in war work that required them to travel to sites not served by bus and rail links. The output of all consumer goods was reduced as the economy moved to the production of armaments.

Overall, industrial production increased only slightly in Britain, but there was a reorienting of activity. Steel and aluminium output increased, for these industries were geared to armaments and aircraft. The output of consumer goods was greatly decreased – it was difficult to replace standard household items: footwear and clothing were rationed.

Efforts were made to find sources of supply of raw materials within the UK. Britain had extensive deposits of low-grade iron ore which had been utilized before the war. Production was increased by 50 per cent as the local source was used to replace imports. Iron railings were cut down and the scrap used for steel-making. Books and newspapers were recycled to reduce timber imports, and state forests, which had been planted in conifers after the First World War, were cut over. Flower gardens were turned into vegetable plots and a ploughing-up campaign brought more land into cultivation.

Changes developed in the countryside. In the 1930s, when prices of agricultural commodities were low worldwide, much farmland in Britain had been allowed to revert to grass and was used as pasture for cattle and sheep. As wartime shipping scarcities impinged on imports more food was grown at home. Between 1939 and 1943, the arable area in the UK increased from 11.9 million acres to 17.9 million acres. Crops of wheat, barley, oats, potatoes and sugar beets increased. As prices for crops were high, land that had been marginal at prewar prices was brought into cultivation.

Livestock numbers decreased overall. As the grazing area for sheep decreased their numbers fell. Pig herds declined as a result of lost imported foodstuffs. Cattle numbers remained roughly steady. Meat production declined, but milk output increased as, in the effort to improve nutritional standards, children were given milk each day at school.

Agriculture had a high priority in the British war effort and was not starved of inputs. Tractor production increased and improved mechanization of farming helped combat the labour shortages caused by conscription.

British trade patterns altered in the war years. British exports shrank and imports grew rapidly. The gap between the value of exports and the value of imports more than doubled between 1938 and 1943. In 1938 Britain got 13 per cent of imports from the United States, its largest trading partner. By 1943 over 40 per cent of imports, by value, came from the US. As a group, Commonwealth countries roughly maintained their share of Britain's imports at around 40 per cent of the total, although the composition of trade altered. Products seen as non-essential, like bananas, ceased to be shipped in favour of basic foodstuffs and industrial raw materials. Imports from Argentina were maintained at around 5 per cent of the total value of all imports. There were no direct imports from France and Germany. In 1938 the two major European economies had each supplied about 3 per cent of the total value of imports into Britain. Neither was as important as Argentina.

Britain came out of the war with some sectors of manufacturing – vehicles, aviation, electronics – strengthened. Overall, however, there had been a lack of capital investment in new equipment, as economic activity was geared to winning the war.

Exports were lost during the war, and it was difficult to reclaim markets after the war. Paying for the huge imbalance of imports over exports had run up overseas debts. The UK ended the war petitioning the US for a loan which it made with tough conditions.[37]

In the immediate postwar years, the British economy recovered slowly and rationing continued. Britain was a manufacturing, trading, banking and shipping country that had worldwide investments. During the war, many of the investments were sold off to pay for imports. When hostilities ceased, shortage of shipping, manufacturing capacity and capital made it difficult to rebuild the trading and financial services networks that had been a key element in the British prewar economy.

In the Second World War, the communists (the USSR), the capitalists (US), the collaborators (France) and the Axis (Germany, Japan and Italy) were agreed on one war aim: they all wanted to dismantle the British Commonwealth. The Soviets coveted British oil interests in the Middle East; the US, as a competitor of Britain in the maritime world, worked to advantage itself economically; the Japanese wanted British markets and raw material sources in Asia; and the Germans and French, when they put together the postwar EC, made sure that the British would pay an entry fee that included dismantling Commonwealth economic links.

THE GREATER EAST ASIA CO-PROSPERITY SPHERE

Japan unified and started to modernize in 1868 with the Meiji restoration. The new central administration adopted policies that favoured industrialization and made direct investments in manufacturing activities. When enterprises became established they were sold on to Japanese investors on favourable terms. The new state quickly began to expand territorially and took in surrounding island groups. In 1895, after war with China, Taiwan was acquired. The island lies on the Tropic of Cancer and became a good source of tropical and subtropical products, including cane sugar and tea. Infrastructure investments were made to exploit the agricultural assets and mineral resources, including coal. After war with Russia (1904) Japan acquired the southern part of Sakkalin island, the Liaotung leasehold and a sphere of influence in southern Manchuria which included the railways the Russians had built. Sakkalin was a source of coal, oil, timber and fish. Korea became a formal colony in 1910 and again capital was put into the ports and railways needed to harvest the agricultural surplus of south Korea and the mineral raw materials of the north.

During the First World War Japan acquired the German Pacific colonies, north of the Equator, the Shantung peninsula, and a more privileged trade position in China. Postwar Japan attended the Washington Naval Conference (1921–2) and signed the arms limitation agreements, but observers like Bywater and Isaiah Bowman[38] saw that Japan intended to continue territorial expansions. In 1931 Manchuria, rich in coal, iron ore and non-ferrous metals, was taken over by military action not planned by the civilian government.

In the 1930s the West became aware of a Japanese form of commercial organization – the *Zaibatsu* (money clique) – which worked to exclude foreign commercial interests from Japan. The British shipping industry was finding it difficult to take cargoes to and from Japan. *Zaibatsu* developed backward and forward economic linkages so that a textile manufacturer might control raw cotton sources, a shipping line, production facilities, retail outlets and financial institutions to fund operations. As a matter of policy a *Zaibatsu* did business with itself wherever possible and this worked against outsiders trying to serve Japanese markets. The *Zaibatsu* was a vehicle for the control of overseas resources and an effective, non-tariff barrier to imports and the activities of foreign investors. In the mid-1930s extensive legislation was passed to support Japanese industry and some of that had the effect of pushing out foreign investment.[39]

In 1937 the Marco Polo bridge incident in China became a war and Japanese forces quickly occupied Beijing, Shanghai, Nanking and other major cities, although the mass of the population, who lived in rural areas, was beyond Japanese control. Now Japan began to employ geopolitical rhetoric and in 1938 the cabinet proclaimed a 'New Order in East Asia', with reference to Japan, China and Manchukuo.[40]

Prewar southeast Asia had received Japanese investment and become an important supplier of iron ore, coal, oil, tin, rubber and many non-ferrous metals to the Japanese economy. There was talk of *nanshin* – advance to the south, although there was no direct military threat to the resource rich regions of southeast Asia which supplied Japan with raw materials.

When Germany overran Western Europe in 1940 the southeast Asian colonies of France and the Netherlands lacked protectors and British defence assets were focused on defending the southeast of England. In August 1940 the Greater East Asia Co-Prosperity Sphere was proclaimed along with pledges to create Asia for the Asiatics. Southeast Asia was to be brought into 'Japan's living space'.[41]

But Japan's actions alarmed the US. On 26 July 1941 Japanese assets in the US were frozen and at the beginning of August an embargo was placed on oil exports to Japan. This made the situation worse. Now the military who wanted a policy of expansion could point to the US restrictions as a reason for taking control of resource rich territory.

In a campaign spectacularly launched by the attack on Pearl Harbor, in December 1941, Japanese forces overran southeast Asia. By the end of April 1942 Japan had occupied or controlled Hong Kong, French Indo-China, Thailand, the Philippines, Guam, Malaya, Singapore, Burma, the Dutch East Indies and many smaller territories.

On the surface Japan had gained, at low cost, a resource-rich region full of strategic minerals and agricultural products like rubber, rice, sugar and tropical hardwoods, including teak. However, the gains were not as glittering as they appeared. For a variety of reasons Japan was able to extract only a small fraction of the resources that she had imported from the region in peacetime. Japan, like Italy, chose the wrong policy and the wrong side. Both countries, because of raw material scarcities at home, had to have access to global markets and maritime routeways. Both countries joined the Axis, embraced the concept of autarky through conquest and lost the war. After the war Japan did establish large-scale economic penetration of the Pacific Rim by skilful investment.

Southeast Asia, the Ukraine and Western Europe presented different problems to occupying forces but in each case it proved difficult to extract the strategic resources. It is one thing to make a profit on an occupation, as Peter Liberman[42] argues happened with the German occupation of Western Europe; it is quite another to integrate the resources of a conquered region into a war economy. Although the godfathers of German geopolitics preached the importance of controlling resource-rich territory, none of them addressed the problems of harnessing raw materials to expanding power in wartime when technical and organizational talents are fully employed running the war machine at home.

None of the geopolitical realms referred to at the beginning of the chapter was to be a clear winner when judged from the year 2000. The Soviet Union made extensive territorial gains at the end of the war but no country paid a higher economic price.[43] Eventually the Soviet model of autarky collapsed. Japan's military and industrial resources were inadequate against the US. The United States finished the war with a greatly enlarged economy and to a degree the US has enlarged the orbit of free trade but the concept of free trade is still far from being accepted worldwide.

The *Mitteleuropa* model of the First World War and the New Order model of the Second World War are the closest to implementation, with Germany as the senior partner in the EU, rather than the hegemonic power. France, Germany, Italy and the Benelux countries had many economic interests in common. During the Second World War they were forced, in straightened circumstances, to interact.[44] After the war, there was peaceable European cooperation with the first movement towards economic integration involving the coal, iron and steel industries – exactly the industries in which there had been the longest and deepest integration under the Nazi regime. As William Rees-Mogg comments:

> From 1940 to 1945, Hitler created a united Europe under German leadership. This not only foreshadowed but made possible the EU which has been created since the war ... Hitler's Europe made the Europe of Brussels possible.[45]

SIX

Planning the Postwar World

There were different views on the form of the postwar world among the allied powers. The Soviet view was starkly geopolitical. The USSR would reclaim the territory lost from the Russian empire at the end of the First World War and establish hegemony over East Europe to create a buffer between the Soviet Union and Germany. In December 1941, with German armies deep in the Soviet Union, the British foreign secretary, Anthony Eden, met Stalin at the Kremlin and was presented with a draft alliance between Britain and the USSR. Britain was asked to agree to postwar Soviet control over Eastern Europe.[1] Stalin wanted much the same deal from Eden as he got from Hitler in August 1939. Britain did not accept the terms of the treaty and Stalin did not alter his views. Beyond the immediate territorial objectives the USSR wanted to spread the Soviet, centrally controlled economic and political model to other parts of the world.

The view from the West was more complicated. President Roosevelt thought that the establishment of a United Nations Organization would provide a mechanism to mediate disputes. It would not be necessary for the US to establish a sphere of influence in Europe, or project power into Eastern Europe. Roosevelt wanted to avoid detailed negotiations about boundaries when the US first entered the war. Cordell Hull told a joint session of Congress on 18 November 1943 that there would be no postwar need for alliances, spheres of influence or other special arrangements.[2]

Some analysts in the State Department and the British Foreign Office, along with commentators such as Walter Lippmann and Nicholas Spykman, saw the dangers of allowing the Soviet Union to reshape the political geography of Eastern Europe, but they were not the policy-makers.

THE ATLANTIC CHARTER

On 9–12 August 1941, a few weeks after Germany had attacked the Soviet Union but before the US and Japan had entered the war, Churchill and Roosevelt met at Placentia Bay, Newfoundland. The leaders arrived on Saturday, 9 August, the Prime Minister aboard HMS *Prince of Wales* and the President in the heavy cruiser USS *Augusta*. That evening Roosevelt said he might be prepared to make a joint declaration of principles. The following day Sir Alexander Cadogan drafted a document which Churchill approved, with alterations. The draft was shown to Roosevelt and there were inputs from Harry Hopkins, Sumner Welles and Averil Harriman. When Cadogan, who had studied Roosevelt's speeches at the Foreign Office, made the initial draft he was clearly careful to include only those concepts and objectives that the American team, representing a neutral power, would be able to accept. There are no specific war aims in the charter other than 'the destruction of Nazi tyranny'. The Atlantic Charter, as the document was called, was made public on 14 August, and contained the following eight principles, which the United States and the United Kingdom agreed to respect:[3]

> First, their countries seek no aggrandizement, territorial or other;
>
> Second, they desire to see no territorial changes that do not accord with the freely expressed wishes of the peoples concerned;
>
> Third, they respect the right of all peoples to choose the form of government under which they will live; and they wish to see sovereign rights and self-government restored to those who have been forcibly deprived of them;
>
> Fourth, they will endeavor, with due respect for their existing obligations, to further the enjoyment by all States, great or small, victor or vanquished, of access, on equal terms, to the trade and the raw materials of the world which are

needed for their economic prosperity;

Fifth, they desire to bring about the fullest collaboration between all nations in the economic field with the object of securing, for all, improved labour standards, economic advancement and social security;

Sixth, after the final destruction of the Nazi tyranny, they hope to see established a peace which will afford to all nations the means of dwelling in safety within their own boundaries, and which will afford assurance that all the men in all the lands may live out their lives in freedom from fear and want;

Seventh, such a peace should enable all men to traverse the high seas and oceans without hindrance;

Eighth, they believe that all of the nations of the world, for realistic as well as spiritual reasons, must come to the abandonment of the use of force. Since no future peace can be maintained if land, sea or air armaments continue to be employed by nations which threaten, or may threaten, aggression outside of their frontiers, they believe, pending the establishment of a wider and permanent system of general security, that the disarmament of such nations is essential. They will likewise aid and encourage all other practicable measures which will lighten for peace-loving peoples the crushing burden of armaments.

On 24 September 1941 the Charter was endorsed by the Soviet Union and the European allies of Britain, although some were hesitant.

On 1 January 1942, 26 nations, including the totalitarian Soviet Union, signed the Atlantic Charter, by then renamed the United Nations Declaration. The United Nations Organization evolved from the declaration, but the first purpose of the signatory states was the defeat of the Axis powers.

The Atlantic Charter is Wilsonian in tone but in contrast to the Fourteen Points it does not mention any place, country or boundary. Britain had gone to war after Poland was invaded in 1939. Poland is not mentioned in the Charter, nor are Czechoslovakia and the Baltic states. These countries and others were left to hope that the right of peoples to choose their own governments would apply to them.

The Charter sets out some globalization principles including equal access to the trade and raw materials of the world (clause 4) and economic collaboration between nations to bring about improved labour standards, economic advancement and social security (5). There should be freedom of navigation on the high seas (7) and force should be abandoned in international affairs (8). Roosevelt's ideas in the Four Freedom speech (6 January 1941) echo in the Charter. Even the reference to 'Nazi tyranny', which Churchill was pleased to see because it was as close as he could get to a US alliance at the time, can be related to Roosevelt's fireside chat of 29 December 1940.

The Charter did not go without criticism. Emery Reves saw that the Charter's emphasis on nations and peoples meant the continued use of the concept of self-determination, as FDR made explicit in a broadcast of 23 February 1942. To Reves self-determination was the principle on which the 1919 world had been built, only to crumble so quickly.[4] Self-determination would lead to the division of the world into more and more states, and would not provide a guarantee of independence nor create an integrated system that would embrace all nations.

What was needed was a Declaration of Interdependence and the development of a concept of international sovereignty which would address international matters.[5] Reves was thinking beyond the nation state to a world where there would be more interaction and interdependence. States would regulate internal matters, in the way US states do, but there would be an international framework for the broader global issues, including individual rights.[6]

ALLIED CONFERENCES

There were numerous conferences involving various combinations of allied powers during the Second World War. Shortly after the US was forced into the war by Japan and Germany, Roosevelt and Churchill decided, at the Arcadia Conference in Washington, DC (22 December 1941–3 January 1942), that the main weight of the available forces would be thrown against Germany, the most dangerous Axis power. At Casablanca (January 1943), the US and Britain agreed that the Axis powers had to surrender 'unconditionally'. At Tehren (28 November–1 December 1943), where the US, the USSR and the UK met, Britain and the United States agreed that Eastern Poland, which the USSR had occupied in September 1939 under the terms of the Soviet Non-Aggression Pact with Germany, should remain part of the Soviet Union after the war. Further, Poland would be moved to the West, taking over German territory, an arrangement which, as G. F. Kennan points out, would leave Poland dependent on the Soviet Union for protection.[7] At Tehren it was generally accepted that Germany would be partitioned, but no detailed plan was laid out.[8] At Yalta (3–11 February 1945) the USSR got agreement that a Soviet-backed group (the Lublin Committee) would form the nucleus of the postwar government of Poland, rather than the London-based Polish government in exile that had continued the war as an ally of Britain.

The Potsdam Conference (17 July–2 August 1945), held shortly after the end of the war in Europe, dealt with the creation of occupation zones in Germany and marked the path towards the division of Germany into the GDR (East Germany) and FRG (West Germany). The conference at Potsdam divided former East Prussia between Poland and the Soviet Union. The Soviet portion included Königsberg and the surrounding territory which was renamed Kaliningrad and incorporated into the Russian Soviet Socialist Republic. Potsdam sanctioned the removal of German populations from Danzig and transferred the port to Poland. In the West, pending the final determination of the boundary, Poland was allowed to occupy German territory up to the line of the River Oder and the western Niesse River. Prewar, all the territories that Poland gained in 1945 – part of East Prussia, Danzig and Lower Silesia – had predominantly German populations. The Potsdam Declaration (2 August 1945) sanctioned 'orderly transfers of German populations' out of Poland, Czechoslovakia and Hungary.[9] In a phrase of today, Potsdam endorsed 'ethnic cleansing', and it was to be far from orderly.

The highly publicized conferences between the UK, the

USA and the USSR were not as important in shaping postwar Europe as is sometimes suggested. The conferences tended to endorse patterns that had already emerged. By Potsdam, the Soviet Union had control of all the territory of prewar Poland, East Prussia, Danzig and Eastern Germany. By the summer of 1945, the Western allies could not alter that fact without the use of force.

NICHOLAS J. SPYKMAN

In 1942, the big picture was that two totalitarian powers were fighting for control of the Heartland. The US was aiding the USSR in the contest against Nazi Germany. If the Soviet Union won it would be the predominant land power in Eurasia. The defeat of Germany and Japan, the flankers that A.T. Mahan wanted to restrain Russian expansion, would increase the potential power of the USSR. Foremost among the commentators who saw the postwar dangers was Nicholas Spykman of Yale University.

Hardly had the United States got into the war than Spykman, addressing a joint meeting of the Association of American Geographers and the Political Science Association in New York on 31 December 1941, suggested that destroying the power of Germany and Japan, countries that had declared war on the US earlier in December, would advance the strategic ambitions of the Soviet Union. This argument was not easily appreciated by an audience[10] still stunned by Japan's day of infamy, and accustomed to Roosevelt's view of Nazi tyranny, to say nothing of propaganda projecting a benign Uncle Joe Stalin.

Spykman had views that were in the Mahan–Mackinder tradition. No one power could be allowed to dominate Eurasia. Thus, shortly after the US joined the Second World War, Spykman was advocating that the form of the postwar world be analysed in terms of power balances, spheres of influence and boundaries. This was not the predominant perspective in the Roosevelt administration.

Nicholas John Spykman was born in Amsterdam in 1893. During the First World War, when the Netherlands were neutral, he served as a foreign correspondent in the Middle East (1913–19) and the Far East (1919–20). After the war, he went to the United States, entered the University of California at Berkeley, and completed degrees in 1921 (AB), 1922 (AM) and 1923 (PhD). After teaching at Berkeley, he moved to Yale in 1925 and organized the Yale Institute of International Studies in 1935.

At the heart of Spykman's ideas was the notion that the United States would have to maintain the balance of power in the postwar world. This view was forcefully set out in *America's Strategy in World Politics: The United States and the Balance of Power*,[11] published in the spring of 1942 and reviewed on the front page of the *New York Times Book Review* on 19 April. The United States had only been in the Second World War for a few months but Spykman had a powerful message: look to the end of the conflict and try to develop power balances which will be advantageous to the United States. America may have been fighting Germany and aiding the Soviet Union, but it was wrong to assume that the destruction of Germany was a good thing and care should be taken not to swing the Eurasian balance of power in favour of Russia, for a Russian state from the Urals to the North Sea could be no great improvement over a German state from the North Sea to the Urals. Similarly, in the Far East, in the effort to destroy Japan it was inadvisable to 'surrender ... the Western Pacific to China or Russia'.[12] Spykman felt that the postwar world order would not differ much from the prewar world and the US had to be prepared to preserve a balance in Europe and Asia. Already he was thinking of the creation of a NATO-like organization, arguing at the University of Virginia on 8 July 1942 for the 'organization of a European power zone with the United States as an extra regional member'. For Spykman the security of the United States 'did not lie in the oceans but in the preservation of the balance of power in Europe'.[13]

Although Spykman came close to describing the policy that the US would eventually adopt after the war, he got no thanks for his views in 1942. When *Life* carried an article on geopolitics and quoted Spykman's views, the magazine got letters criticizing the geopolitical approach.[14] In response, Spykman argued that 'Justice is most likely to prevail among states of approximately equal strength, and democracy can be safe only in a world in which the growth of unbalanced power can be effectively prevented.'[15]

After the publication of *America's Strategy*, Spykman became ill, dying in 1943 at the age of 49. Shortly after his death *The Geography of Peace* was published, advancing the idea that the rimland (equivalent to Mackinder's marginal crescent) was the key strategic region in world affairs.

> The rimland of the Eurasian land mass must be viewed as an intermediate region, situated as it is between the heartland and the marginal seas. It functions as a vast buffer zone of conflict between sea power and land power. Looking in both directions, it must function amphibiously and defend itself on land and sea. In the past, it has had to fight against the land power of the heartland and against the sea power of the off-shore islands of Great Britain and Japan. Its amphibious nature lies at the basis of its security problems.[16]

Spykman, by the end of his life, had developed a view of the world which was to become dominant in American foreign policy in the Cold War era. The US would hold a balance, develop regional security arrangements and support states on the margin of Eurasia against takeover by a Heartland power. Spykman was a prescient commentator but not the author of containment policy.

ALEXANDER P. DE SEVERSKY

One of the most popular books on strategy to appear in 1942 was de Seversky's *Victory Through Air Power*.[17] De Seversky argued that air power had become the major element in overall strategy and he illustrated his point with examples. In the battle for neutral Norway in May–June 1940, the British attempt to help Norway repulse the German invaders failed because of air power. The German invaders were supported by land-based planes flying from Germany, Denmark and, very early in the campaign, Norway. British Hurricanes and Spitfires lacked the range to operate from bases in Eastern England over Norway and carrier-based aircraft could not match the performance of land-based *Luftwaffe* planes. Although the Royal Navy was far superior to the German navy, and the latter lost half its destroyer force in actions on the coast of Norway against the British navy, the overall result of the Norwegian campaign was determined by superior air power.[18]

In de Seversky's view, the evacuation of nearly 300,000 British and French troops from Dunkirk (1940) was possible because the Royal Air Force, flying from bases in southern England, could prevent the *Luftwaffe* from establishing air superiority over the evacuation zone filled with waiting columns of troops and small boats ferrying them to offshore transports. The air battle at Dunkirk indicated that the *Luftwaffe* would not be able to establish air superiority over the English Channel and, therefore, a German invasion of Britain would not be possible.

The catalogue of actions in which air power had altered the balance was impressive. The Royal Navy could not use the base at Malta if Axis air forces dominated the skies above the island from Sicily; the British lost their foothold in Greece and Crete in April 1941 because of inadequate air power;[19] the *Bismarck* was sunk 27 May 1941 because it lacked air cover, as were the *Prince of Wales* and *Repulse* off Malaya.[20] Germany had not defeated the Soviet Union in the autumn of 1941 because the bases necessary for air power could not be created fast enough behind the initial successful advance.[21]

The Second World War revealed that some slogans concerning air power were myths, including: the bomber will always get through and civilian populations will be demoralized by aerial attack. Major de Seversky argued that the random bombing of cities was a poor use of air power, pointing out that 'unplanned vandalism from the air' must give way to attacks on objectives like electricity-generating plants, aviation industries and transportation facilities.[22] The British and American airforces in 1942 were using pattern bombing strategies and the annihilation of cities, which postwar bomb damage surveys showed were an uneconomical use of air power.

De Seversky argued that air power had replaced sea power and that the US could organize air supremacy[23] over the world from the US. *Victory Through Air Power* prepared American readers for the idea that the US, if it were to be a major world power, had to have a strategic air force. De Seversky argued for postwar global involvement by the US and described the means of projecting power from air bases and aviation industries in the US.

THE 'GEOPOLITICAL' LITERATURE OF 1942

Many books on grand strategy, geopolitics and the form of the postwar world appeared in 1942. It was a year in which all major magazines and many academic journals carried articles on geopolitics. Some of the articles were of high quality, utilized excellent maps and opened the reading public in the US to a global view and a sense of the major regions that make up the world.

A number of books analysed the ideas of Karl Haushofer and other German geopoliticians. Robert Strausz-Hupé in *Geopolitics: The Struggle for Space and Power* gave a chilling account of the German view of geopolitics. The First World War had resulted in the end of the old European civilization and begun a new age of global struggle in which the strong states would compete to create power blocs under their domination. The weak states would be subordinated by the dominant states by whatever means proved effective.[24] Hans W. Weigert, in *Generals and Geographers: The Twilight of Geopolitics*, analysed the differing viewpoints within German geopolitics and Derwent Whittlesey, with the help of Charles Colby and Richard Hartshorne, set out the *German Strategy for World Conquest*.[25]

In addition to the new books and articles, several classics were reissued. Halford Mackinder's *Democratic Ideals and Reality* reappeared, and Douhet's *Il Dominio del' Aria* (Rome, 1921) was translated into English and published as *The Command of the Air* in 1942.[26]

WALTER LIPPMANN

Walter Lippmann was a widely read and incisive commentator on world affairs. He had worked for the Inquiry and, in the years after the First World War, favoured a Wilsonian view of international affairs.

With the outbreak of the Second World War in Europe, Lippmann saw a threat to the US unless the country engaged the aggressors before the war reached the Western hemisphere. Far from seeing President Roosevelt in 1941 as a shrewd politician edging the public towards the war, Lippmann thought that FDR was engaging in verbal defence, not putting the industrial capacity of the US on a war footing and encouraging the view that Germany could be defeated without sacrifice or inconvenience.[27] Further, Lippmann attacked the isolationists who believed that an armed circle could be drawn around the United States. In Lippmann's opinion, all countries had soft sides and the US had two. The Atlantic was narrow in the north and the US could be attacked via a series of island stepping stones – Britain, Ireland, Iceland and Greenland – leading to Canada, a numerically small nation on the northern flank of the US. In the south, the Atlantic was narrow between Africa and Brazil and there was a danger of fascist takeovers in Latin American countries which would expose the US from the southern flank.[28]

In 1943 Lippmann published *US Foreign Policy: Shield of the Republic*. In the introduction Lippmann acknowledged that he was abandoning many previously held views. The US needed a more engaged foreign policy. Echoing Spykman, Lippmann declared that:

> The Atlantic Ocean is not the frontier between Europe and the Americas. It is the inland sea of a community of nations allied with one another by geography, history, and vital necessity.[29]

The members of the Atlantic community were: France, Spain, Portugal, the Netherlands, Belgium, Denmark and Norway, in addition to the United Kingdom and the United States.[30] The great question concerning Europe was: Would Russia extend her power westward to threaten the security of the Atlantic states? Lippmann thought there was going to be an expansion of Soviet influence in Central and Eastern Europe. Britain and the US could not maintain a settlement in the region by military force. The countries of East Europe were weak and even in an alliance among themselves, against the Soviet Union, the US would be incapable of supporting the smaller countries against the greater power. Further, if the Red Army liberated Eastern and Central Europe, it was inconceivable that the governments in exile would be allowed to return and establish anti-Soviet states on the borders of the USSR. The question to be settled was: Would the Soviet Union allow the pre-war countries of Eastern and Central Europe *to exist as independent states*?

Lippmann thought the way to avoid a confrontation in the centre of Europe, a confrontation that would set the stage for a Third World War, was to neutralize the countries of the region. Lippmann had a realistic view of the degree of power that the US and the UK would be able to project into the centre of Europe at the end of the war. He hoped that the USSR–USA–UK alliance would continue after the war, within a new order of states, but he saw that in the event of disagreement over the status of the countries that lay between the Soviet Union and Germany, the US and the UK would be unable to contest the issue.[31]

In 1944 Lippmann published *US War Aims*, in which he suggested again the creation of an Atlantic Community, while the Soviets were allowed to control Eastern and Central Europe. The Islamic and Hindu countries should form their own regional systems. In *War Aims* Lippmann laid down an important principle: Japan should not be allowed to hold the balance of power in the Far East and Germany should not hold the balance between the Atlantic Community and the Soviet orbit. In practice, this was going to mean that Germany had to be bound into Western Europe and Japan allied with the United States.[32]

UNCONDITIONAL SURRENDER

At the Casablanca meeting (January 1943), attended by Churchill and Roosevelt, a policy of unconditional surrender was adopted for Germany, Italy and Japan. There would be no negotiations on the form of the peace prior to surrender.

Additionally, no allied power would make a separate peace with any of the Axis countries.

The policy of unconditional surrender was aimed at avoiding a mistake of the First World War. After the Versailles treaty was signed, there was a widespread view in Germany that the country had not been given a treaty in accordance with the Fourteen Points. This view was debatable from several perspectives, but to make certain, the second time around, that Germany would understand that the country had lost the war and was not being offered any concessions to get her into peace talks, a policy of unconditional surrender was adopted.[33]

However, there were disadvantages to a policy of unconditional surrender. It gave the Axis powers little option but to fight until they were overwhelmed and it had large territorial implications. A policy of unconditional surrender meant that the anti-Axis powers were going to occupy the territory of Germany, Italy and Japan. In practice, the Western allies invaded Italy and occupied a part of that country when it sued for peace in 1943. Germany took control of the remainder. Japan surrendered in 1945 to be occupied principally by US forces, although the Soviet Union declared war late against Japan, breaking the USSR–Japan Non-Aggression Pact of April 1941, and occupied, and retained, several strategic islands including Sakhalin and the Kuril islands. The effect was to push Soviet territorial waters out into the Pacific and to seal off the northern approaches to Japan.

CREATING A POSTWAR GERMANY

Occupation meant responsibility for administering and running the economy of enemy territory. As the economies of the Axis countries collapsed at the end of the war, the occupying powers took over devastated lands and the responsibility of feeding the defeated populations. The need to get economies going again forced the Western allies to utilize many existing economic structures and help them survive into the postwar world. Industrialists, managers, companies and economic structures closely associated with the war regimes in Italy,

Germany and Japan contributed to the so-called economic miracles in the postwar era.[34]

Italy made peace in 1943 and many of the institutions and state corporations established under Mussolini contributed to postwar recovery. Austria was declared a victim of Nazi aggression and, after a period of occupation, was given an independent, neutral status. Although Hitler was Austrian, the degree to which Austrians had contributed to the work of the Reich was not fully examined at the time. The major problem was Germany, and a debate developed in the West over what territory Germany should be allowed to retain and what to do with the Germans who lay outside that territory. Sir Halford Mackinder wanted Germany 'embanked' by the allies so that the Germans could make no further trouble.[35] There were many other plans, some of them drastic.[36]

THE MORGENTHAU PLAN

In 1944, the US was prepared to restructure Germany radically. At the Quebec Conference between Britain and the US in September 1944, Roosevelt and Churchill accepted the Morgenthau plan, drafted by the Secretary of the US Treasury. Henry Morgenthau subsequently published his official memo, with additional commentary, as a book, *Germany Is Our Problem*.[37]

Morgenthau wanted to deindustrialize Germany, divide it into three and detach territory that would be transferred to France and Poland (illus. 10). The details were that East Prussia would be divided between the Soviet Union and Poland. Danzig would go to Poland, as would the upper course of the River Oder, containing the cities of Breslau and Oppeln. In the West the Saar region, with the coalfield, would be transferred to France.

What remained of Germany would be cut into three sections: a north German state, a south German state in a customs union with an Austria restored to its 1938 boundaries, and an international zone on the Rhine running north from Mainz to the North Sea and Denmark that would include the Rhur.

Morgenthau wanted to transfer German territory to surrounding states and he wanted to move Germans from the lost

10 Morgenthau's division of Germany.

territories into a diminished Germany. Many in British and US foreign policy circles thought cutting Germany down in size and packing refugees into the smaller national territory would cause long-term problems. The Germans would never accept the proposed partition and Britain and America would not enforce it over a period of years.[38] The British Treasury did not believe that 'deindustrializing' Germany was in the long-term economic interests of the United Kingdom.[39]

The economic aspects of the Morgenthau plan are most frequently referred to today. The Ruhr industrial region was, in the words of the 1944 memorandum, to be 'stripped of all presently existing industries' and so weakened, that it cannot 'in the foreseeable future become an industrial area ... All equipment shall be removed from the mines and the mines closed.'[40]

Closing the mines was impractical, for the Ruhr produced nearly half of the coal mined in Western Europe. In 1945 the British coal industry was not producing enough coal for British needs and would not be able to supply traditional, prewar markets in Denmark, the Netherlands and France. The treatment of the Ruhr coal industry was modified in Morgenthau's book (1945). The Germans of the Ruhr were to be removed, but coal was to be mined by a replacement population of French, Belgian and Dutch workers, and the region placed under a governing body established by the United Nations.[41]

Where had the Morgenthau plan come from? The idea of separating the Ruhr from Germany was suggested by Jean Monnet at a lunch with Stimson early in 1944.[42] Stimson did not like the idea[43] but he shared it with Morgenthau. Morgenthau and his staff worked up strong arguments showing, correctly, that prewar Germany by controlling external trade using cartels, currency controls and bilateral agreements had been a comparatively small trade partner with the countries of Western Europe.[44] These facts were used effectively to get Roosevelt to accept the Morgenthau plan.

The flaw in the plan was the proposal to close the Ruhr mines, which Morgenthau dropped in 1945. Monnet would know that France wanted access to Ruhr coal. Everyone else should have known that Western Europe could not run without Ruhr coal.

Whatever the background, Morgenthau, by focusing on the Ruhr, had highlighted the geopolitical problem that was central to a stable postwar settlement. The coalfields of Europe are not evenly distributed. A huge proportion of the coal reserves are in the Ruhr, and the Ruhr has most of the coking coal supplies needed for steel-making. Belgium, Luxembourg and France have sources of iron ore but lack sufficient coal. German steel-makers had abundant coal and access to high-quality Swedish iron ore. On this basis the Ruhr became the largest steel-making region in Europe, because German steel-makers had lower costs. Matters could be kept that way as long as French steel-makers could be made to pay more for coal inputs than German steel-makers.

France liked Morgenthau's ideas of internationalizing the Ruhr and wanted the region to be supervised by Britain, France, Belgium and Luxembourg. The international authority would allocate the coal and France would get a share that would allow

French steel-making capacity to be increased at the expense of Germany. The industrial centre of gravity would shift from Germany to France.[45] Here was model A of the European Coal and Steel Community.

Late in 1945 France pressed strongly in London, Washington and Moscow to have the Ruhr made a separate state. Britain and the US did limit production of German steel and other products after the Second World War and did allocate Ruhr coal across Europe but they were not prepared to create a separate Ruhr state.[46] In the end the best that France and Monnet could get was the European Coal and Steel Community (1951) which eventually created a more rational distribution of iron and steel production in Western Europe.

THE SUMNER WELLES SCHEME

In *The Time for Decision*, Sumner Welles suggested boundary alterations and the division of Germany.[47] Sumner Welles would have transferred East Prussia to Poland, and Germany would have been partially compensated by the movement eastward of its Eastern boundary to include areas that, prewar, had contained substantial German populations. In this scheme, the Polish corridor and East Prussia were to be eliminated. Sumner Welles would then have divided Germany into three separate states:

(a) South Germany including Bavaria, the Rhineland, and the Saar (Morgenthau would have transferred the Saar to France);

(b) a Western state containing Hanover, Westphalia, and Saxony; and

(c) an Eastern state consisting of Pomerania, Brandenburg, and Silesia (Morgenthau would have transferred Silesia to Poland, and the Soviets did see that the region was incorporated in Poland).

Sumner Welles wanted to establish a European customs union. The three German states he proposed would be allowed to join the union. Germany, under the Welles plan, would be split into three regions that could interact economically; political power would be decentralized, but Germany would be integrated into the European economy. Already, those in US policy-making circles were seeing a customs union as a way to integrate Europe and bind Germany into Europe.

The Sumner Welles plan, with its ideas of European economic integration, contains elements that did emerge in the postwar world. Like Morgenthau, Welles favoured the transfer of populations to bring ethnic distributions into conformity with international boundaries.

The Western allies did not adopt a coherent territorial policy concerning Germany, and by the end of the war the reality was that the Soviet Union controlled, by force of arms, the lands that had made up East Prussia, the port of Danzig and the surrounding territory, all of Poland including the Polish corridor and Eastern Germany. The Soviet plan was simple. Eastern Poland would become part of the Soviet Union. Poland and the USSR would each get part of East Prussia. Poland would acquire Danzig and, in the West, prewar Germany up to the Oder–Niesse line. All persons of German ethnic background would be expelled from East Prussia, Danzig, the former corridor and the lands up to the River Oder. There was a mass expulsion of ethnic Germans in which the forced migrants left behind possessions including land, homes and household goods. The human and economic cost was borne all across East Europe as large areas of farmland were depopulated and the former German inhabitants of Poland, Czechoslovakia and Hungary were forced into a Germany decreased in size. There were food shortages in East Europe, Germany and Western Europe as Britain, France and the US struggled to feed enlarged populations in their occupation zones in Germany.

As the international boundaries and ethnic distributions of Eastern Europe were rearranged, the Soviets began to reshape political structures. Moscow-orientated communists were placed in positions of advantage from which they could take control of countries as the war ended. For example, the London

Polish government in exile was ignored by Moscow as the Lublin government took over the country. Polish politicians returning from London were arrested and charged with high crimes. Eastern Europe was saved from the jaws of Nazi Germany only to be swallowed into a Stalinist, Soviet empire.

SEVEN

The Cold War and the
Triumph of Geopolitics

American leaders in the Second World War, Roosevelt and Cordell Hull, thought that there would be no need for alliances and spheres of influence when the war ended. However, having been forced to support a totalitarian empire – the Soviet Union – against the totalitarian empire of Nazi Germany, the leaders were wrong to think that geopolitics would end with the war. The seeds of the Cold War sprouted on Midsummer's Night, 1941, as the Axis attacked the USSR and the US moved to support Stalin and his regime. As the war ended the 'strategic space of geopolitics became ... global'.[1] Quickly the postwar world was divided into blocs: a Western bloc led by the United States and a communist bloc dominated by the Soviet Union in Europe and by China in East Asia. The blocs were ready for war. NATO, established in 1949, provided for the defence of Western Europe and North America. The Warsaw pact (1955) was formed as a result of German rearmament which had been a response to the Korean War, as American Pacific demands increased and she needed more help in Europe. Communist China wanted to attack Taiwan but was deterred by the US Pacific fleet.

The blocs competed for global influence. The West promoted democratic political systems but was prepared to ally with dictators so long as they proclaimed anti-communism. The Soviet Union tried to export its economic model to Latin America, Africa and Asia. The Chinese were less influential but converted some countries, including Albania, to their brand of communism. In every continent civil wars were fought between communists and Western-aided groups for control of countries and political systems. Among the most visible of the wars were conflicts in El Salvador, Nicaragua, Angola and Vietnam.

The blocs precipitated one crisis after another: the Berlin blockade, the Korean war, Suez, the Hungarian uprising, the U-2 flights, the Cuban missile crisis, the Prague Spring, the Arab–Israeli wars, the Vietnam war, the invasion of Afghanistan, the arms build-up of the 1980s, the fall of the Berlin Wall and German unification – any one of these geopolitical events might have led to conflict involving both superpowers.

After the Second World War Eastern Europe was restructured. The middle-tier states had been economically aligned to Germany. Now Germany was divided into occupation zones and doing little international business. Eastern Europe was taken over by the Soviet Union and reorientated politically and economically. The boundaries of the region were redrawn from top to bottom. Finland gave up land in Karelia and 400,000 Finns living there had to be absorbed into the smaller country. In the north, Finland lost contact with the Arctic Ocean and the ice-free port of Petsamo was taken by the Soviets, who also acquired a direct land boundary with Norway.

The Baltic states, taken into the USSR in 1940, did not reappear until the Soviet Union broke up. Poland lost territory to the Soviet Socialist Republic of the Ukraine in the east and, at Potsdam, East Prussia was divided between the Soviet Union and Poland. The Soviets took the ice-free port of Königsberg with the surrounding territory, renaming the city and the region Kaliningrad. Poland got the southern and western portions of East Prussia, together with the Baltic port of Gdánsk (Danzig). Lithuania, now in the USSR, got Memel once more, renaming the port Klaipèda. The German populations of Königsberg, Danzig and Memel fled or were forced out.

As Poland, territorially, moved to the west the Polish corridor disappeared. At Potsdam Poland was allocated extensive tracts of Pomerania and Silesia, which prewar were undoubtedly inhabited by Germans. Stalin had told the Western allies that the German population had fled Pomerania and Silesia. This was never wholly true and when the fighting stopped, many Germans returned to their towns, villages and farmsteads,[2] but the 'Poles were determined to do unto the Germans as they had been done by', and expelled German populations to gain a secure hold on the territories.[3] Some forced

11 Boundaries of European states, *c.* 1950.

migrations were organized, but often Germans in Poland, or what had become Polish territory, were ordered out of their homes with half an hour's notice and forced on to the road west. Observers recorded that the forced migrants were peasants, and the majority of them were either elderly or children. Many died of starvation or illness, for the migrants lived on what they carried. Little was provided along the way.[4]

The Sudetenland Germans, who numbered more than three million people, were expelled out of fear that, once Germany recovered, the ethnic German population would be exploited to destabilize Czechoslovakia as had happened in 1938. There were German communities in Romania, Yugoslavia and Hungary.[5] There were wholesale expulsions from Yugoslavia, occupied by Germany in the Second World War. The exodus from Hungary and Romania was smaller as those countries had been allies of Germany.

Europe was awash with forced migrants, or displaced persons, as they were termed. Hungary and Czechoslovakia exchanged ethnic populations. Italians were forced out of towns at the head of the Adriatic, taken over by Yugoslavia. Soviet citizens, including prisoners of war, who found themselves in the West were forcibly repatriated, although it was known they were likely to be shot or sent to Siberia.

Before the Second World War, the Soviet Union did not have borders with Lithuania, Czechoslovakia or Hungary (illus. 6). The pushing westward of the Soviet–Polish border and the division of the territory of former East Prussia between the two states gave the USSR a direct border with Lithuania, now a Soviet Socialist Republic.

A Czechoslovak-Soviet treaty of 29 June 1945 transferred the province of Subcarpathian Rus' to the USSR where it became Transcarpathia within the Ukraine SSR. There were ethnic arguments in favour of the transfer, but the territory had not been a part of the Russian empire and when the USSR got Subcarpathian Rus', it acquired direct borders with Czechoslovakia and Hungary, a situation which had not previously existed (illus. 11). The direct borders facilitated Soviet intervention in Hungarian and Czechoslovak affairs as happened in 1956 and 1968, respectively.[6] As the name implies, the Transcarpathian region straddles the Carpathian mountain range, and the transfer of the territory improved the land defenses of the Soviet Union by giving it control of the Uzhok, Torun, and Tatar mountain passes.

In 1940, Romania had been forced to cede a large segment of Bessarabia and northern Bukovina to the Soviet Union.[7] Romania briefly regained the territory when it joined Germany in the attack upon the Soviet Union in June 1941. At the end of the war the USSR restructured the boundary. The Bukovina, with half a million inhabitants, was incorporated into the Ukraine. Bessarabia, with a population of 3.2 million, was incorporated into a Moldavian Soviet Socialist Republic, and part of the region merged into the Ukraine which was enlarged along the Black Sea shore to the Danube delta, where the

Soviets took the port of Izmail. Romania also gave up territory on the Black Sea shore to Bulgaria.

Overall, Romania lost a substantial part of its Black Sea frontage. The Soviet Union acquired a large area of coastal lowlands with a relatively mild climate and high agricultural potential. The area became an important producer of grapes, tobacco, sunflowers and many other crops for the Soviet Union. In spite of its huge land area, a relatively small proportion of the USSR consisted of good agricultural land. The gains at the expense of Romania were important in this context.

In addition to taking territory from Finland, Estonia, Latvia, Lithuania, Poland, Czechoslovakia and Romania, the Soviets were one of the four powers to have an occupation zone in Germany. The Soviet occupation zone was to become the GDR (East Germany), a client state of the USSR. The Soviets had an occupation zone in Austria which included the capital, Vienna. In addition, the Red Army occupied Bulgaria, never at war with the Soviet Union, and supported the communists in the Greek civil war. As perceptive commentators in late 1944 and early 1945 had feared, Europe was being 'bisected into two spheres of influence'.[8]

ECONOMIC CONSEQUENCES OF THE WAR

> From the Channel ports to Stalingrad stretches territory devastated by modern war, its industries laid waste, its fields largely uncultivated, devoid of transport facilities or communications and inhabited by a new race of troglodyte shelter-dwellers.[9]

Anyone travelling in Europe in the months after the war ended was appalled by the devastation, the disruption and the hordes of displaced persons. The devastation was not confined to Germany. France had been heavily bombed to disrupt transportation before, during and after the Normandy landings of June 1944. Belgium and the Netherlands were not quickly liberated after the invasion. German forces held on in Antwerp and in most of the Netherlands, as the allies advanced towards the Rhine. In the central Netherlands, where the cities of Rotterdam, Amsterdam, Leiden and Utrecht are located, starvation conditions existed with the population reduced to eating tulip bulbs if they could get them.[10] In the north, the Royal Air Force bombed dikes to let in water to harass the German defenders, who in turn breached dikes to impede allied ground forces. In many towns and cities, death rates more than doubled in 1944 and early 1945 as inhabitants lost 15–20 per cent of their body weight.[11] Between 1939 and 1945 in the Netherlands, the crude death rate per thousand of the population went from 8.6 in 1939 to 15.3 in 1945.

Conditions were better in Norway where the population was generally well fed and clothed and timber provided a plentiful fuel supply.[12]

The damage done to Germany by bombers based in Britain was massive. In 1941, 1942 and 1943, although strategic manufacturing plants were attacked, the greatest weight of bombs was dropped on city centres. In spite of the bombing, German armament production increased in 1942, 1943 and the first part of 1944. Then US and British bombers changed their aiming points. Railroad stations and marshalling yards were targeted for attack. In addition canals that carried bulk cargoes of coal and raw materials and strategic road and rail bridges were bombed. Eventually coal, steel and components could not be moved around the country and the manufacturing sector of the German war machine began to disintegrate.[13]

When observers from Britain reached Germany after the war, they were overwhelmed by sights of 'utter destruction' in all the larger towns. Hamburg, Kiel, Frankfurt and Berlin were 'little more than heaps of rubble', in which the inhabitants lived in basements beneath the ruins. Food, housing and heat were short.[14]

In the smaller towns and country areas, people were housed, fed and clothed, but the centres of all the large cities had to be rebuilt. At Cologne bulldozers cut lanes through the rubble to create alleys for the inhabitants to walk along. Eighty-five per cent of the city was uninhabitable and all five bridges across the Rhine had been destroyed by air attacks or charges set by the retreating *Wehrmacht*.

The most badly damaged city in Europe was Warsaw. It was

bombed and fought over in the German attack of September 1939. In April 1943 the Jewish ghetto was obliterated and when the Poles rose up against the German occupation in 1944, the city was systematically destroyed by German forces. In 1939 Warsaw had a million inhabitants. By 1946 the population had been reduced to 300,000. Half the prewar population had been killed off, others had fled the city. The bridges across the Vistula were destroyed, and there were no whole buildings in the central part of the city. From the east, Warsaw formed a low, black, uneven mass against the sunset. No lights shone from the ruins. 'Warsaw was a city of darkness.'[15]

German transportation systems had been disrupted and segments of manufacturing capacity destroyed by bombing. In addition, basic, primary sector industries like coal mining and farming had run down due to shortages of labour, equipment and maintenance.

In Britain, farming became more productive in the war years.[16] In Germany, conscription removed farm workers who were replaced by foreign, forced labour. Output declined and as hostilities ended, the forced labour left. In areas that were fought over, farm buildings, equipment and livestock were destroyed. Land was left unsown in the spring of 1945.

Coal production had slumped all across Europe by the end of the war. In 1938 the UK produced 235m tons of coal. By 1945 the figure was 186m tons. Production had decreased in Germany and for that country the problem was made worse by the transfer of the Saar coal mines to France and, in the east, the loss of mines to Poland and the inability to move coal out of the Soviet occupation zone in East Germany. In 1937 Germany produced 158m tons of hard coal. In 1946 production was down to less than 60m tons of hard coal in the western and eastern sectors of the country.

Prewar, the Ruhr had supplied nearly half of Western Europe's coal. Now the Ruhr could not meet those needs as shortages of labour and transportation curtailed production.[17] The same was true in Britain. In 1938 the UK was a major coal exporter. By 1945 the British coal industry could not supply the UK as an ageing and declining workforce struggled to maintain production in mines from which the best coal had been cut. In the summer of 1945, in the months after VE Day, it became obvious that there would be fuel crises in Europe during the winters of 1945–6, 1946–7 and 1947–8.

Today it is difficult to appreciate the importance of coal in the European economy, half a century ago. Coal had been the fuel of the European industrial revolutions. By 1945 the North Sea oil and gasfields had not been found. Coal was the major fuel and mining coal was a major industry in Europe. Coal supplied fuel for the dense rail networks that carried a high proportion of the freight moving in European countries. Most long-distance passenger traffic moved by rail. Homes were heated by coal, electricity was generated with coal, iron was smelted with coal. A coal shortage would impede economic recovery.

In most of Europe, the supply of food and fuel got worse after the defeat of Germany. Many people struggled through the winter of 1945–6 on food rations at, or below, starvation levels. Housing was short due to war damage and the cessation of the construction of homes over a six-year period. There was not enough coal to provide adequate heat and electricity (Table 3).

In the following winter, 1946–7, the weather made things worse. Normally, Western Europe has mild winters as the westerly wind system imports warmth, cloud and rain from the Gulf of Mexico. Spells of freezing weather, associated with easterly winds blowing out of the cold high pressure system that dominates the interior of Eurasia in the winter, are usually short. In the early months of 1947 there was a long, unbroken spell of freezing weather. From Britain to Poland, coal mines could not meet the demand for fuel. Factories closed, the generation of electricity was curtailed, homes were cold and often unlit.

In 1945 and 1946 Europe was facing a fuel and food shortage, and basic industries struggled (Table 4). Infant mortality rates rose alarmingly at the end of the war in parts of Europe and did not come down rapidly. In March 1946, there was a report that the infant mortality rate, in the British occupation zone of Germany, was more than twice the prewar figure, at the rate of 170 per thousand live births. Table 5 shows the trends. One of the more sensitive indicators of living standards is the infant mortality rate – the number of children per

Table 3 Coal production, selected countries, 1939–46
(figures in million metric tons).

	1939	1945	1946
Germany (hard coal)	188.0	166.0 (1944)	53.9*
France	50.2	35.0	49.3
UK	235.0	186.0	193.0
Belgium	29.8	15.8	23.0
Netherlands (hard coal)	12.9	5.1	8.3
Czechoslovakia (hard coal)	16.8 (1937)	23.2 (1944)	14.2
Italy (hard coal)	1.1	0.1	0.1

* West Germany only

Note: The German figure is for hard coal only, and excludes lower-quality brown coal which was also mined in large quantities. The French figure for 1946 reflects the gain of the Saar mines. Czechoslovakia mined 25 million tons of hard coal in 1943.

Source: Mitchell (1998).

Table 4 Crude steel production, selected countries, 1939–46
(figures in million metric tons).

	1939	1945	1946
Austria	0.780	0.172	0.187
Belgium	3.1	0.729	2.3
Czechoslovakia	2.4	0.993	1.7
France	7.9	1.7	4.4
Germany	23.7	18.3 (1944)	2.6*
UK	13.4	12.0	12.9

* East and West Germany

Source: Mitchell (1998).

thousand live births who do not survive the first year of life. In conditions where food, warmth and shelter are scarce, the smallest and weakest die first. At the end of the war, infant mortality rates rose substantially in many countries. In Austria and the Netherlands, the rate more than doubled the prewar figure.

Table 5 Infant mortality, birth rates, and death rates in Europe, 1939 and 1945.

	1939			1945		
	IM	BR	DR	IM	BR	DR
Austria	73	20.7	15.3	162	15.9[B]	13.4[B]
Belgium	82	15.0	13.2	100	15.3	14.5
Denmark	58	17.8	10.1	48	23.5	10.5
France	68	14.6	15.3	114	16.2	16.1
Germany	72	20.4	12.3	97[*B]	16.1[*B]	13.0[*B]
Italy	97	23.6	13.4	103	18.3	13.6
Netherlands	34	20.6	8.6	80	22.6	15.3
Norway	37	15.8	10.1	36	20.0	9.7
England and Wales	51	14.8	12.1	46	15.9	12.6
Spain (non-belligerent)	135	16.5	18.4	85	23.1	12.2
Sweden (non-belligerent)	40	15.4	11.5	30	20.4	10.8
Switzerland (non-belligerent)	43	15.2	11.8	41	20.1	11.6
Czechoslovakia	98	18.6	13.3	137	19.5	17.8
Poland	140[A]	24.3	13.7	N/A	22.8	13.4[B]
Hungary	121	19.4	13.5	169	18.7	23.4
Romania	176	28.3	18.6	188	19.6	20.0

[A] 1938, [B] 1946, [*] West Germany only

Source: Mitchell (1998).

In the desperate postwar efforts to restart the mines and industries of the Ruhr, little effort was made at denazification. Generally speaking, 'the managers and foremen of Nazi days' were retained in power and there was little change in the social order with the liberation of Germany. Leading industrialists were arrested, but the day-to-day management of mines and factories was still in the hands of people intimately linked into the Nazi regime.[18]

When the Second World War started, most of Europe was still farmed in traditional ways. Farming units were small family operations. The family supplied much of the labour. Mechanization was limited by shortage of capital and the small size of agricultural holdings. A great part of farm activities was devoted to producing food for the farm family. To produce a comfortable subsistence, a great variety of crops and livestock was needed. Most farms kept hens, cattle, pigs and sheep to provide eggs, beef, milk, butter, ham and mutton. Horses or oxen provided the power to pull the plough. Oats were grown to feed horses, turnips were raised as fodder for cattle and sheep. Around the farmhouse and barnyard, orchards and kitchen gardens produced fruit and vegetables. Family farms produced small surpluses of crops and livestock for local markets. Even in areas where there were large land holdings, as in much of East Europe, production methods were inefficient. Large estates employed large labour forces at low wages. The labourers could hardly subsist on the wages and the estates could not produce efficiently for they lacked mechanization and chemical inputs.

There was efficient farming in Denmark, the Netherlands and parts of Belgium, France and Germany, but after six years of war, none of the better farmed areas had remained efficient. The vineyards of France and Germany did not yield as many grapes or as many bottles of wine. The intensive livestock and arable areas of mainland Europe had run down as a result of diminished inputs and reduced mechanization. In the traditional, labour-intensive farming regions, lack of manpower reduced production. Let us examine traditional farming in East, Central and Western Europe using Poland, Germany and France as examples.

At the end of the war, although Poland lost land in the east to the Soviet Union, it gained farmland in East Prussia, Lower Silesia and Pomerania at the expense of Germany. Poland did not need additional farmland – it needed more machinery and fertilizer to intensify agriculture. As it was, the land taken over from Germany was not sown in 1945 and produced little in

1946. In the areas fought over, near the prewar German border, there were no livestock, few people and hardly a farmhouse or farm building undamaged.

By contrast, in central Poland the crops planted in the spring of 1945 were harvested in the summer, and the winter wheat and the winter rye were sown in the autumn. But even in this area, livestock numbers were down compared with the prewar figures. Cattle herds were half their former size, pigs and horses at 25 per cent, and flocks of sheep had nearly disappeared with only 10 per cent of the prewar numbers being present.

By the end of 1945 in Poland, many of the large estates were subdivided into small peasant holdings of about 12 acres. Such small units were incapable of mechanization. They would not give peasant farmers a good living and they were too small to produce marketable surpluses of crops. Few understood, at the time, that the break-up of the estates into peasant units was a political step on the road to the creation of collective farms.

Prior to the Second World War, Poland had exported food; now food production was inadequate. Infant mortality had risen to almost famine levels, and tuberculosis was on the rise. Poland had less than half the doctors it possessed in 1939, as a result of the closing of medical schools, deaths of doctors in war zones and the deliberate effort of both Germany and the Soviet Union to kill off the educated classes in Poland. A significant proportion of the Poles found in the mass grave at Katyn, in western Russia, systematically killed by the Soviets, were reserve officers with medical training.

In 1939 Germany produced 80 per cent of the food consumed by the population. In 1944 the national territory was a war zone, the harvest was far below normal and all the men in rural areas – even the old and young teenagers – were pressed into defence units.

During the war, German farming had every incentive to increase production a totalitarian regime could provide – except inputs of fertilizer and equipment. The chemical and vehicle industries were engaged in war work. Tanks before tractors, explosives before fertilizers, was the rule. As labour was drawn from farms to the *Wehrmacht*, agricultural production fell. In 1939 Germany grew 5 million metric tons of wheat; by 1944 the harvest was down to 3.8 million metric tons. Fifty million tons of potatoes were grown in 1939. Less than 40 million tons of potatoes were lifted in 1944.

As the war ended, there were large losses of agricultural land to Poland in East Prussia, Pomerania and Silesia. The agricultural production of the Soviet occupation zone in the east was lost to the remainder of Germany. This was important, for prior to the war the great industrial areas, including the Ruhr, were in the West and drew upon the agricultural surplus of the eastern part of the country.

In the Soviet occupation zone of Germany, farms and estates were split into 10-hectare peasant holdings, again as a step towards the collectivization of agriculture. In the western occupation zones Germans were provided with a minimum food ration. The UK struggled to feed the population in its zone and had to cut food rations in Britain to do so.

The problems of European agriculture, in general, are revealed by looking at the case of France. Overall, farms in France were small in size, usually less than twenty acres, and composed of scattered land holdings. A third of the workforce was in farming, there was little mechanization, output per acre was low and productivity per worker was poor. There were few machines for milking cows and, a century after the development of reaping machines, most harvests were brought in by hand. Tractors were few, most ploughing was done by horses, or bullocks, pulling single-furrow ploughs. Combined seed and fertilizer drills were unknown, and some seeds were still broadcast by hand.[19]

France had pre-industrial farming. Production had dropped during the war and would partially recover with the return of labourers to the land. The establishment of modern farming would require larger, consolidated farms, mechanization, chemical inputs, improved varieties of seed and specialization of production at the expense of the great range of crops and livestock that most small, subsistence farms produced in an uneconomical way. Specialized, profitable farming was possible, as French vineyards indicated.

Inefficient postwar agriculture was to be transformed by

European Economic Community policies. The economic growth that the EEC helped sustain allowed many to leave jobs as farm labourers, or move off small-holdings to take better-paying jobs in urban areas. EEC agricultural policies paid high prices for agricultural produce and made it profitable to increase production. To produce more, with less labour, farms had to invest in more land, mechanization and chemical inputs and, if the investments were made and more produced, the Common Agricultural Policy – the CAP – guaranteed a market and paid above world price levels for agricultural commodities. The CAP was a product of the old desire for autarky, the remembrance of wartime scarcities and the immediate postwar fear of famine. There was also the political reality that in a Europe largely farmed by peasant farmers, the European idea could be sold more easily in traditional rural areas by linking a European community to higher farm prices.

The end of the Second World War did not bring political stability to Europe. Britain and the Scandinavian countries returned rapidly to normal, as did the Netherlands. In France, the government of General de Gaulle went quickly. Spain was still under a fascist regime led by General Franco. Italy, like France, fell into a pattern of short-lived coalition governments that rarely survived for more than a few months. Germany was run by armies of occupation.

The USSR did not try immediately to impose communist rule on the countries of East Europe, at the end of the war. First, an interim government acceptable to the Soviet Union was established that declared itself willing to include cabinet members from other parties. Once in office, the interim governments secured control of the instruments of power and one-party communist rule emerged. Communists suspected of being nationalists, as opposed to being totally committed to Moscow doctrine, were purged from communist governments. It took several years for the interim governments to be replaced by communist governments subservient to Moscow, but by February 1948 and the overthrow of democratic government in Czechoslovakia, all of Eastern Europe was under Soviet control.

The economic consequences of Soviet hegemony were huge. Prewar, all the countries of East Europe had important trade links with Germany. During the war, the economic links had been strengthened. Now trade with Germany was cut off. New, centrally planned economies were developed and external trade diverted to the Soviet Union or other communist East European countries.

The Second World War resulted in widespread destruction, both in East and West Europe. There was a war of attrition on the Russian front that led to widespread, systematic destruction on the way into the Soviet Union, and on the long retreat of the *Wehrmacht* back to Berlin. In the West, towns, communications and industrial capacity were bombed until they ceased to function. As they retreated, German forces devastated territory as it was given up.

In the occupation zones of Britain and the US, the commanders worked to get the economy functional. It quickly became apparent that the skills, technical knowledge and expertise still existed. Western Europe had lost physical assets but not the ability to rebuild and operate advanced industrial plant. If political stability could be secured and capital provided, the region could be prosperous again. Economically, countries were not so devastated as they looked.[20] Industrial production rebounded rapidly and reconstruction stimulated economic growth.[21] Postwar investment levels were high.[22]

The pace of recovery was slower in Eastern Europe and the Soviet occupation zone of Germany suffered as assets were removed. In what became West Germany recovery was rapid, the allies needing to get their zones economically active, or provide foodstuffs and subsidies to the defeated inhabitants. The resources of the Saar were utilized in the French economy. The US armies of occupation encouraged industrialists to repair plants and get production going again in their zone. Resources were provided to help this happen. In the British occupation zone German prisoners of war were put to work in the agricultural sector – operation Barleycorn – and the industrial plant was restarted. The Volkswagen plant at Wolfsburg was taken over by British military engineers, and by 1946 was producing 1,000 cars a month. At first the cars were supplied to allied forces but by 1947 production was up to 2,500 cars a month and exports started. A German manufacturing director was appointed in 1949 and the company handed over to the West German government. The Volkswagen miracle was driven by the British need to get the economy going in their zone or pay the bills.[23]

THE COLD WAR

To the geopolitical commentator the roots of the Cold War were apparent in 1941. Once the battle for control of Eurasia started between Germany and Soviet Union, there could be two results. The combatants might exhaust each other as Truman famously hoped in 1941 or one of the powers would be preponderant in Eurasia. When Britain and the US became allies of the Soviet Union, to prevent a German empire from the North Sea to the Urals, they had joined a cause in which victory *would* bring a westward extension of Soviet power. A second front would be needed to ensure that the Soviets did not occupy all of Germany up to the Rhine.

In retrospect it is obvious that there would be conflict between the totalitarian, communist regime of Joseph Stalin that wanted to extend its power into Eastern Europe and the US which wanted democratic governments and increased economic interaction. The differing world views were rapidly reflected in postwar despatches sent by diplomats serving in Washington and Moscow.

When the Soviet ambassador to the US, Nikolai Novikov, sent his long telegram on 27 September 1946, he described America's outward push into the world in Marxist terms:

> The foreign policy of the United States, which reflects the imperialist tendencies of American monopolistic capitalism, is characterized in the postwar period by a striving for world supremacy.[24]

Novikov noted the build-up of US overseas bases and saw that the US was intent on opening the world to US trade and investment, while promoting the dollar as the currency of world trade.

From the US and British perspective the Soviet Union, in spite of signing the Atlantic Charter and the UN declaration, had indulged in territorial aggrandizement in Eastern Europe. Opinion moved rapidly towards a tougher policy in regards to the USSR. In February 1946 George Kennan despatched his long telegram from Moscow to Washington and on 5 March, on the campus of Westminster College in Fulton, Missouri, with President Truman present, Winston Churchill delivered his famous speech that contained the phrase 'From Stettin in the Baltic to Trieste in the Adriatic an iron curtain has descended across the continent.'[25]

In the long winter of 1946–7 the British economy contracted, factories closed, exports declined, coal had to be imported and the international balance of payments problem became critical. At the end of February 1947 the British government informed the US that it could no longer provide aid to Greece and Turkey, countries subject to Soviet threat. If they came under Soviet control, it was feared that Soviet influence would spread into the Middle East and Africa.[26] On 12 March 1947 President Truman told a joint session of congress that the US would 'support free peoples who were resisting attempted subjugation by armed minorities or by outside pressures'.

In July 1947, *Foreign Affairs* published an article entitled 'The Sources of Soviet Conduct'.[27] The anonymous writer 'X' was George Kennan and he suggested that the US should adopt 'a policy of firm containment, designed to confront the Russians with unalterable counter-force at every point where they show signs of encroaching upon the interests of a peaceful and a stable world'.[28] Further, Kennan made the remarkable prophesy, since fulfilled, that the Soviet Union carried within it 'the seeds of its own decay, and that the sprouting of these seeds is well advanced'.[29]

The policy of containment, as stated in the 1947 article, lacked a geography. There was no reference to where the policy might have to be applied. There was no regional weighing of the overseas interests of the US. This aspect of containment, as stated by Kennan, was quickly commented on by Lippmann,[30] who saw that on the Eurasian continent it would be impossible to meet the Soviet expansion at all points. If the

US committed to contain the USSR everywhere, then the US would concede the strategic initiative and allow the USSR to choose the points, on the margins of Eurasia, where it would challenge the US.

Lippmann maintained his earlier view that the natural allies of the United States were the nations of the Atlantic community for the 'Atlantic Ocean and the Mediterranean Sea, which is an arm of the Atlantic Ocean, unite them in a common strategic, economic, and cultural system'.[31] The chief components of the Atlantic community, in addition to the US, were the British Commonwealth, the Latin states on both sides of the Atlantic, Scandinavia, Belgium, the Netherlands and Switzerland. Lippmann was wary of binding Western Germany into the Atlantic community for he thought the Soviet Union would have the power to detach Germany from the Western allies in the future. The inducement to Germany would be an offer to partition Poland again and the return to Germany of Silesia and other former German territory that the country lost at the end of the First and Second World Wars.

THE MARSHALL PLAN

The Truman Doctrine and the policy of containment addressed the issue of Soviet expansion but did not deal with the perceived economic weakness of Europe. The winter of 1946–7 crippled Britain economically and brought Germany to the verge of starvation. Farming in France had not recovered, and the harvest of 1947 was poor. If economic recovery failed, communism might find it easy to come to Western Europe.

Secretary of State George Marshall, in a speech at Harvard University on 5 June 1947, suggested that the US would support Europe economically, if the Europeans could come up with a programme of economic cooperation. The Marshall Plan was open to the Soviet Union and the countries of Eastern Europe if they wished. Marshall's speech was not given great prominence in the United States, but European journalists stationed in Washington were alerted to the importance of it and their reports produced a reaction in Britain.[32]

Britain, France and the Soviet Union met in Paris, 27 June–3 July 1947, to discuss a European response to Marshall's idea. As the US wanted the countries of Europe to come up with their own ideas, the United States was not formally represented at the conference. Britain and France saw the need to establish a European framework to take advantage of the Marshall Plan. The Soviet Union wished only to send a list of needs and requests for aid to Washington.

As the debate went on, it became clear that the Soviet Union was not going to join the Marshall Plan,[33] and the British Foreign Secretary whispered to one of his advisors that they were witnessing 'the birth of the Western bloc'.[34]

In spite of Soviet obstruction, a conference on European Reconstruction convened in Paris on 12 July 1947 and with this conference, the geography of the Cold War began to emerge. Twenty-two countries were invited to the conference by Britain and France. Italy, the Netherlands, Belgium, Denmark, Luxembourg, Iceland, Norway, Austria, Greece, Portugal, Switzerland, Sweden, Turkey and Eire accepted. Germany and Spain were not invited. Bulgaria, Poland, Czechoslovakia, Finland, Hungary, Romania and Yugoslavia declined their invitations under pressure from the Soviet Union. The USSR saw that the Marshall Plan would project US economic influence into Europe and would strengthen the role of the dollar as the world's major trading currency. If the Soviet Union and the East European countries joined the Marshall Plan, they would become part of a trade area dominated by the US.[35] It is now recognized that the Marshall Plan was part of a process by which the US 'sought to restructure the world economy'[36] to promote international economic integration and ensure that the US had access to economic space in Europe.

The Paris Conference on European Reconstruction led to the creation of the Organization for European Economic Cooperation (OEEC).[37] The US provided funding under the Foreign Assistance Act (2 April 1948), and established the Economic Cooperation Administration to work with OEEC. From the establishment of OEEC in the autumn of 1947, Europe began to divide into Eastern and Western blocs. At first the alignment of the blocs was economic not military.

The year 1948 resulted in more steps towards the creation of a European community. On 17 March 1948, Britain, France, Belgium, the Netherlands and Luxembourg signed the Brussels Treaty which promoted economic cooperation and collective defence. In the following month, the Convention for European Economic Cooperation was signed by the sixteen nations participating in the Marshall Plan. The Convention (16 April 1948) suggested the establishment of a European Customs Union. In June the London Agreement on the Future of Germany envisaged the association of Germany in the European economy.

Eventually, the Marshall Plan produced many positive developments and promoted institutions of economic cooperation out of which the European Economic Community emerged. But in 1947 and 1948 fear of the Soviet Union was the force bringing about cooperation. The British Foreign Secretary, Ernest Bevin, who had been a leading figure in developing the Brussels Treaty, realized that in the event of a Soviet attack, the signatory states of the Brussels Treaty – Britain, France and the Benelux countries – could not resist effectively. Bevin persuaded his European partners and the US of the need to create a North Atlantic defensive alliance.

THE NORTH ATLANTIC TREATY ORGANIZATION

On 4 April 1949, the US, the UK, France and the Benelux countries together with Canada, Italy, Denmark, Iceland, Norway and Portugal signed the North Atlantic Treaty in which they agreed that an armed attack against one or more of them in Europe or North America would be considered an attack against all of them. Kennan was against the NATO concept. He did not endorse the concept of perimeter defence, set out in NSC-68 (1950).[38] Nevertheless, NATO became the foundation of Western defence.[39] It was the first and most important of a series of regional defence agreements which the US fostered and joined. In 1951 a peace treaty was signed with Japan, and the US entered into a defence arrangement that allowed it to station forces there. Together with bases in Okinawa, Guam and the Philippines, with which the US signed a security treaty in 1951, the US created a line of strong points off the Pacific shore of Asia. In 1951 the US signed a mutual defence pact with Australia and New Zealand – the ANZUS Treaty. In 1955, SEATO (South East Asian Treaty Organization) was established. Australia, New Zealand, the US, UK, France, the Philippines, Pakistan and Thailand joined the organization. The US was never a full member of CENTO, the Central Treaty Organization created by the Baghdad Pact (1955), but did give security guarantees to Turkey, Pakistan and Iran, who were members along with Britain.[40]

By the mid-1950s, the perimeter of Eurasia (Mackinder's marginal crescent, Spykman's rimland) was ringed with treaty organizations and defence agreements designed to contain the spread of communism, the expansion of the Soviet Union and the perceived imperial aims of mainland China. The global defence map looked like the plan sketched by Spykman in *American Strategy*. The US was a part of many entangling alliances. However, it was not the treaty organizations that got the US into trouble, but rather the philosophy of containment, a dread of the spread of communism, and simplistic ideas like the 'domino theory'.[41]

SOVIET-DOMINATED EUROPE

In October 1947 the USSR established the Cominform to promote cooperation between communist parties in Poland, Yugoslavia, Bulgaria, Romania, Hungary, Czechoslovakia, the Soviet Union, Italy and France. Yugoslavia broke with the organization in 1948, but in the following year, the Council for Mutual Economic Assistance (Comecon) was founded with six members – the Soviet Union, Bulgaria, Czechoslovakia, Hungary, Poland and Romania. The German Democratic Republic (East Germany) was admitted in 1950 and later Mongolia, Cuba and Vietnam became members. The aim of Comecon was to promote 'the development of socialist economic integration'.

The Warsaw Pact was established on 14 May 1955 to provide a unified military command for the forces of the Soviet Union,

Poland, Czechoslovakia, East Germany, Hungary, Romania, and Bulgaria. Like NATO, if one member was attacked, the other signatory states would act together against the aggression.

By the mid-1950s, Europe was divided into blocs on the basis of political philosophy, economic organization, and military alliances. West Germany was rearmed, a NATO member and a forward base for American aircraft. East Germany was part of Comecon and the Warsaw Pact.

The process of dividing into camps was not confined to Europe. The former Japanese colony of Korea was divided into a communist north and a US-orientated south. The communists won the civil war in China in 1949, and the nationalists retreated to Taiwan (Formosa). The US protected Taiwan and other offshore islands like Quoymoy from attack. After the defeat of the French at Dien Bien Phu (1954), Vietnam was divided. North Vietnam was ruled by the communists and an independent government was established in the south that looked to the West for support.

The Soviet Union gained influence in the Middle East after agreeing to supply arms to Egypt in 1956. The arms deal led to the withdrawal of a promise of funding for the Aswan High Dam. In response, the president of Egypt, Colonel Nasser, nationalized the Suez Canal. The Suez Canal company was French, and the British government was a major shareholder. Britain and France then invaded the canal zone. Under UN resolutions, supported by both the US and the USSR, Britain and France were forced to evacuate the canal zone. Soviet influence in the region expanded with Syria and Iraq obtaining arms from Eastern bloc sources.

In 1959 Castro took over in Cuba and by 1962 was prepared to allow Soviet missiles, aimed at the US, to be based in the island. The vessels carrying the Soviet missiles and other military supplies were turned back by US action, but Castro went on to attempt the export of revolution to several Central American countries and Bolivia. The conflict between the superpowers spread into Africa with opposing sides in civil wars receiving arms from the West or the Soviet bloc.

Discipline was not perfect within either bloc. Yugoslavia broke with the Soviet Union, although retaining a communist regime, in 1948. In 1953 there was widespread unrest in East Germany which was ruthlessly put down, as was the Hungarian effort to depose the communist government in 1956. Soviet tanks were again used to keep a communist government in place in Czechoslovakia in 1968.

In the Western bloc, France was never an easy ally and in 1966, although remaining a member of NATO, removed its forces from the command structure of the alliance and had NATO installations taken off French soil.

In their efforts to control large segments of earth space, the superpowers allowed themselves to be drawn into foreign wars that should have been avoided. In the 1950s, during an era of rabid anti-communism in the US, the defence policy of the country was committed to containing not only the Soviet Union, but the spread of communism. By the 1950s political and military leaders were using a domino theory in which the fall of one country to communism would lead to a knock-on effect with surrounding countries falling like a set of dominoes. Thinking of this type led the US to support South Vietnam against takeover by the North. US forces were used in the Vietnam war and suffered 50,000 deaths. Eventually, the involvement could not be sustained politically and forces were withdrawn. South Vietnam was taken over by the North and became part of the Socialist Republic of Vietnam in 1976. The Southeast Asian 'dominoes' of Malaysia, Thailand, Burma and Indonesia did not fall.

Soviet forces were drawn into a war in Afghanistan in 1979. Here, too, there were large losses of men and equipment, and Soviet forces withdrew in 1989. The civil war continued without Soviet assistance.

By the mid-1980s the old colonial empires had largely gone. The desire for confrontation between the superpowers was declining. There was an awareness that the costs of defence spending was more than the US and the USSR could bear. The appearance of Paul Kennedy's *Rise and Fall of Great Powers* in 1987 summarized the mood of an age. Kennedy argued that great powers declined because they overextended themselves territorially and financially. Decline was ushered in not by defeat but by default as resources were overcommitted in the pursuit of empire.[42] The USSR and the US may not have possessed old-fashioned overseas empires, but they had worldwide commitments,[43] and the cost of maintaining an armed global reach was becoming prohibitive. The US gave up bases, as in the Philippines, and reduced the number of units stationed overseas to support treaty commitments like NATO. As the USSR relaxed its grip in Eastern Europe, old nationalist forces, contained by the Cold War, began to exert themselves. Czechoslovakia split, Yugoslavia shattered and the Soviet Union, which contained many distinct ethnic, religious and language groups, disintegrated.

By the time the USSR broke into pieces, the concept of centrally planned and controlled economies was discredited. The way forward was to open national territory to outside investment, innovation and competition. If industries could not compete then let the consumer buy cheaper, imported products and move the displaced labour and resources into other activities.

Western Europe, since the 1950s, had been moving towards porous borders between countries with regard to trade, capital and labour. In 1989 free trade was initiated between Canada and the United States, and Mexico was shortly to join the North American Free Trade Area. Deregulation, the acceptance of foreign investment, the reduction of tariffs, and the privatization of state-owned industries were ideas that gained acceptance in many regions of the world.

Why had it taken so long? The Great Exhibition of 1851, opened as Britain adopted a policy of free trade, had displayed commodities and manufactured goods from all around the world. A few years later an even more ambitious exhibition opened in Paris. By 1872 Thomas Cook was organizing world tours and Jules Verne's *Around the World in Eighty Days* (1873) sold hugely in France, Britain and America over many years.[44] The basic technologies of railroads, steamships, telegraphs, telephones, electricity, refrigeration, automobiles, wireless communication, aeroplanes and film-making were all developed before the First World War.

In *Anticipations* (1902) H. G. Wells described how the existing technology would develop and allow a high degree of global connectivity.[45] In 1900 all the economic mechanisms used today in the globalization process were being practised.

Britain had benefited from a policy of free trade. Germany had created a customs union which had been peaceably expanded to include Luxembourg. The empire of Austria-Hungary had common economic policies, a customs union and a common currency. A network of commercial treaties was beginning to bring tariffs down in many parts of Europe.[46] But the desire to control space made it difficult for statesmen to think of cooperation. McKinley imposed stiffer tariffs at just the time the US was becoming an economic superpower. Germany benefited from Britain's free-trade policies before the First World War and exports to British markets were increasing strongly with a balance of trade in Germany's favour. This did not stop Germany wanting to acquire a larger, formal empire.[47]

Joseph Chamberlain split all the political parties in Britain with his call for protectionism ('tariff reform') in 1903. He failed at the time but had laid the foundations for the system of imperial preference tariffs adopted in 1931–2.[48]

To a degree Britain had a globalized economy before the First World War but just as soon as sustained economic competition emerged, from the US and Germany, Britain became defensive and an opportunity to develop more economic cooperation passed. Statesmen of the era thought in terms of British, German or American interests and that translated into policies that sought to control earth space. Populations were largely uneducated and conditioned to think territorially and nationally. Many statesmen could understand Mahan's idea that a North Atlantic community[49] was the way forward and the leaders of that community would be Germany, Britain and the United States, but politically the concept was too great a jump. There was no shortage of ideas. H. G. Wells and others saw the need for global political institutions. The intellectual origins of the League of Nations are found in the prewar era. Norman Angel in *The Great Illusion* (1909) argued that war between industrial states was unprofitable. But Angel saw that populations, bound up in nationalist loyalties and subject to 'the crowd mind', could be easily led to disaster and difficult to guide to a global view.[50]

When Mahan wrote of his North Atlantic community he expressed the view that France was unlikely to provide leadership and, in fact, France tended 'to lie outside the community of North Atlantic states'.[51] However, two world wars shuffled the pieces on the game board in new ways. After the Second World War it was France, a protectionist, bureaucratized state, that shaped the foundations of the European Economic Community, which has evolved to become the EU and plays a major role in the global trade system. The protectionist biases of the EU are kept in check by the US, for no economic power can function efficiently without access to the markets and financial institutions of North America.

EIGHT

Globalization and the Death of Geopolitics?

The Second World War was good for the economies of North America. Manufacturing had grown rapidly in the United States, Canada and Mexico and the economies were more inter-linked. Canada became the most important trade partner of the US, and Mexico became a major partner (Table 6). The seeds of NAFTA were sown by the Second World War.

However, apart from some small economies including Australia, New Zealand and Sweden, North America was alone in experiencing sustained economic growth (Table 7). As the war ended the question for the US became whether it would be possible to sustain economic growth or would the end of wartime production would result in industrial contraction and a prolonged recession. Observers in the Soviet Union thought there would be another crisis of capitalism as the war ceased to provide economic stimulus. It was clear in the US that more overseas markets would have to be opened up and there were unfounded hopes of enlarged trade with China and the USSR. Many thought that the countries of the British Commonwealth could be lucrative markets now that Britain was weak and short of shipping and goods to export. There were those who wanted to press US commercial interests hard, at the expense of Britain. The reality was, however, that Britain had been the largest export market for the US before and during the war. Britain was by far the most important transatlantic market and many goods shipped to Britain were re-exported to Europe. Canada's trade with Britain was also large and many Canadian exports incorporated components manufactured in the US. If Britain slumped there would be an impact on the economy of Canada that would be transmitted to the US.

Table 6 Destination of US exports in millions of dollars.

	Canada	France	Germany	Japan	Mexico	UK
1938	468	134	107	240	62	521
1946	1,442	709	83	102	505	855
1950	2,039	475	441	418	526	548

Note: In every year quoted, with every trading partner, the US had a favourable balance of trade, exporting more by value than was imported.

Source: Mitchell (1998).

Table 7 Index of manufacturing production.

	US	USSR	UK	Canada	Mexico	Japan	Belgium
1938	100	104	97.3	100	100	63	81
1939	–	–	–	–	–	–	–
1940	–	–	–	–	–	–	–
1944	287	–	–	234	138	79	–
1945	–	–	–	–	–	–	–
1946	–	–	99.7	–	–	17	73

	Denmark	France	Germany	Italy	Nether-lands	Norway	Sweden
1938	100	92	113	100	100	100	110
1939	–	–	–	–	–	–	–
1940	–	–	–	–	–	–	–
1944	88	35*	125	–	–	–	–
1945	–	–	–	29	31	57	113
1946	–	–	–	–	–	–	–

* Excludes Alsace-Lorraine.

Source: Mitchell (1998).

Clearly a top priority for US economic policy was to help get the economy of the UK back on a peacetime footing as one of the engines of world trade. At Bretton Woods (1944) the sterling area was given a place in the postwar financial world and the creation of the International Monetary Fund provided resources that would help smooth balance-of-payment problems. In 1945 the US made a large loan in an effort to revitalize the British economy, although there were tough conditions including making the pound sterling convertible and the ending of imperial preference.[1]

At the end of the Second World War it became clear that China, engaged in a civil war, was not going to be an immediate market for US goods and that the Soviet Union was not going to buy much from the US. European countries embarking on reconstruction were a ready market and there was a postwar export boom to France, as needed equipment was bought by French industry. Few European countries had reserves of dollars with which to pay for US goods and it was not easy to sell products to the US, to earn dollars, because the US still had high tariffs.

As Spykman had predicted, the postwar order had many similarities to the prewar world. One similarity was that most of America's major overseas trade partners were in Europe. If the US economy was to enjoy export growth then one way or another, the economies of West European countries had to grow and be made more accessible to US products. It is against this background that the Marshall Plan emerged; the plan avoided a mistake made after the First World War when the US took money out of Europe and helped stall economic growth. The Marshall Plan put funds into Europe and helped accelerate the economic recovery that was taking place.

The Marshall Plan would stimulate growth but how were US goods to gain easier entry to Europe? Officials in the State Department had talked throughout the war of creating a European customs union (CU). In general the State Department wanted to see the creation of a customs union that would remove impediments to trade between the states of Europe and establish common tariffs on all goods entering Europe. This would make it easier for US corporations exporting to Europe.

The precise form of a European customs union is not usually spelt out in memoirs and nobody fully understood the distinction between a customs union and a common market.

Countries can form various types of international trade groups. In a free trade association the members create free trade among themselves but are free to trade with non-members on terms of their own choosing. A customs union creates free trade between the member states and erects a common external tariff on goods entering the CU from non-members.

In a common market the members develop free trade with each other, erect a common external tariff, work towards the creation of common business conditions and adopt many common policies. These distinctions were not made in the immediate postwar discussions concerning a European customs union and the term had different meanings in the minds of those involved. Acheson told Bevin that he wanted the free movement of goods, labour and capital in Europe but he did not place much emphasis on the common external tariff that a CU would employ.[2]

When President Truman spoke on foreign economic policy at Baylor University on 6 March 1947 he set out the general direction of policy. The US was not proposing or offering free trade but it was prepared to negotiate with other parties to create freer trade and use the Reciprocal Trade Agreement Act for that purpose. Probably it was intended, by the Truman administration, that Europe would create a CU with a unified, and simplified, tariff system and then the US would negotiate to create freer trade between itself and the European customs group.[3]

What eventually emerged from Europe was an economic community – the Common Market – which had a common external tariff (a protective device) and common statist policies including the common agricultural policy (CAP) designed to subsidize European farmers and discriminate against agricultural imports from North America and elsewhere. The Common Market cannot have been what US policy-makers were thinking of in the years 1943–50 if their intention was to help US farm exports.

US policy-makers did not consider in the immediate postwar era the protectionist histories of France, Germany and Italy, nor did they understand the degree to which statist policies were favoured by European bureaucrats. Coudenhove-Kalergi, the visionary who kept the European union idea alight in the totalitarian era, approved of state intervention in economic affairs.

In the immediate postwar years, 1945–8, Britain could have taken the lead in shaping a Europe that cooperated economically, while moving towards freer trade but avoiding the creation of a bureaucracy of control. Ernest Bevin, the foreign secretary, was in favour of a customs union that included Britain, Europe, Commonwealth countries and the overseas territories of the Netherlands, France and Belgium. The external tariff, the tariff on goods entering from non-members, would be low.[4] The addition of other countries would be relatively easy because new entrants would not have to accept numerous common regulations on entry. All of which would have been compatible with the ideas of US policy-makers.

The problem was that Britain would not take the lead. For a variety of reasons Bevin had few supporters for his scheme in the Cabinet. It was pointed out, correctly, that British trade was not mainly with Europe. In 1948, as in prewar years, none of Britain's top six trade partners was in Europe. There was a fear that the Commonwealth, collectively a trade partner second only to the US, would be disadvantaged, and Commonwealth countries were owed a debt for their part in the Second World War.

The Labour government, elected in 1945, had a large programme of legislation. The top priorities were health, education, housing and living standards in Britain. European trade arrangements were not an immediate political priority. Further, the Attlee government was adopting statist economic policies, nationalizing the coal, rail and steel industries – the commanding heights of the economy, in socialist jargon. Nationalized industries were going to be nurtured by government and shielded from the type of competition that would emerge within a customs union, with no barriers to trade between members.

Bevin's vision was met by a general failure of other ministers and ministries to look ahead and appreciate that European unity in some form was coming and once a European economic community was established Britain would be disadvantaged if she was on the outside. The chance for Britain to shape a Europe bound together by encouraging freer trade relationships slipped away. The European, regulated integration that did emerge had a history that included Napoleon's continental system, the German *Zollverein*, Hollweg's European economic association and Mussolini's corporatist state. The origins of the EU can be found in Europe's geopolitical past rather than in the late nineteenth-century tradition of free-trade globalization.

The first institution of economic integration was the European Coal and Steel Community. The coal, iron and steel industries had developed cross-border integration in the years prior to the First World War[5] but in general were seen, at a governmental level, as an arena for geopolitical competition.

As we have seen, in the spring of 1944, Jean Monnet suggested that the Ruhr be separated from Germany and internationalized.[6] The idea passed to Morgenthau, who proposed closing the Ruhr mines.[7] Europe could not be run without Ruhr coal, but France liked the idea of a separate Ruhr and late in 1945 France proposed that the Ruhr be turned into an international state with its own currency and customs and the coal production allocated across Europe by an international commission.[8] Until 1948 a French aim was to weaken Germany but in that year Monnet, after a visit to the US and talks with Dean Acheson and George Ball, developed the idea of a European coal and steel community. If France could not control the Saar and the Ruhr then the best thing to do was to bind German heavy industry within a European structure.

Not all countries were in favour of the coal and steel community. The Belgian coal industry had mined the best seams and was expensive. Germany feared that France was still trying to control German coal and French steel producers did not want to be in direct competition with German steel mills. Making steel in Italy cost twice as much as it did in France or Germany. Luxembourg saw the advantage of cheaper German coal and the Netherlands, with small coal and steel industries, was an enthusiastic supporter.[9]

Britain, with recently nationalized coal and steel industries, did not want to join an organization in which a supranational authority, in an effort to form a rational distribution of coal and steel production in Europe, would decide where new investments were made. Politically it was almost impossible to have a debate if one question was going to be 'Were British lads going to be made redundant by German miners and steel workers?' But the issue was decided without input from Britain. The coal and steel community – the Schuman plan – was announced on 9 May 1950. The communiqué declared that the old oppositions were to be eliminated by placing French and German coal and steel production under a common higher authority. Other countries could join if they wished.[10]

Here was the desired Franco-German *rapprochement* but developed in a form that made it clear that the new partners would plan the future of a Europe that would be regulated and statist. The coal and steel community was phased in over a period of years and in the long run made the region better able to adjust to the structural changes that have taken place globally in the coal and steel industries.

Once the six – France, Germany, Italy, Belgium, the Netherlands and Luxembourg – agreed on the coal and steel community, progress was rapid. The Messina conference in 1955 laid the groundwork for the European Economic Community and in 1957 the Treaty of Rome, designed to promote the free movement of labour, capital and goods, came into force, along with a common external, protective tariff. Britain resisted joining the community but was now faced with the reality that the community existed and the UK was on the wrong side of the tariff barriers. Too late Britain developed a European Free Trade Association but the other members – Switzerland, Sweden, Austria, Portugal, Norway and Denmark – had relatively small economies. Geographically EFTA was peripheral to the core of Europe, which was dominated by the territory of the six members of the EEC.

The European Community did not expand in the period when de Gaulle was using the Common Market as 'an exclusionary device to direct European trade in the interest of France'[11] but when de Gaulle left the scene, after rejecting British applications for membership twice, the UK, Denmark and Ireland joined the EEC in 1973. Norway, having negotiated membership, voted, in a national referendum, not to join. In the 1980s much of southern Europe came in: Greece (1981); Spain

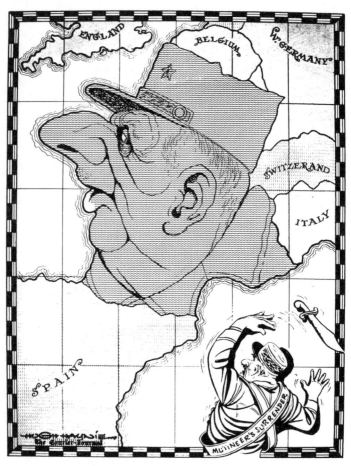

4.26.61

All Gaul Is United Into One Part

12 The General said 'Non' ... referring to the UK's application to the EEC.

and Portugal in 1986; Sweden, Finland and Austria were admitted in 1995; Poland, the Czech republic and Hungary are about to enter. In 1992 EFTA and the EEC agreed to region-wide free trade involving members of both organizations.

Europe has opened up many channels for trade between countries of the region. But the EU still retains structures of its geopolitical past. As one observer has noted:

Today, instead of serving as a catalyst for economic growth through free trade, the EU is focusing inward, promoting trade among its members but raising walls against the rest of the world.[12]

The achievements of the European Community are large. Many impediments to trade have been removed between the countries of Europe. A multinational corporation can set up operations, in Italy for example, and sell into the territory of all EU members. Many, but not all, obstacles to the free movement of labour and capital have been removed. A start has been made on providing the community with a common currency, which will give a uniform price base and not be subject to exchange costs on movement across the borders of member states.

When US policy-makers pushed for European unity at the end of the Second World War they thought they were on the path to making European markets more accessible to American corporations as part of a general process of opening up trade on a global basis. For US businesses to enjoy better access to Europe the obvious next step is a free-trade agreement between the EU and NAFTA.

At the time the Common Market was created it was assumed by some American commentators to be a step on the way to a free-trade arrangement which would include Britain and the US.[13] The assumption was one of the reasons that de Gaulle blocked British entry into the Community in the 1960s (illus. 12). In turn NAFTA can be enlarged to include the countries of Latin America, beyond Mexico. Historically, France, the Netherlands, Britain, Spain, Portugal, Italy and Germany have had commercial links with Latin America and the Caribbean and there are many opportunities to increase trade between Europe and the Western hemisphere.

Latin America illustrates the problems weaker players have coming to terms with economic globalization. After the Second World War the Economic Commission for Latin America, ECLA, developed the idea of import substitution. It was believed that Latin American countries were largely producers of foodstuffs and industrial raw materials. If manufacturing was to develop and replace imported products, the home market would have to be protected.

Although import substitution did create jobs in the manufacturing sector, eventually the policy became discredited as protected producers turned out high-cost, low-quality goods in an economic environment regulated by bureaucrats rather than by competition in the marketplace. At one point Brazil virtually banned the import of computers. This did not produce a vibrant Brazilian industry and denied the country access to the best computer technology.

After the Second World War Latin American governments tended to have nationalist economic policies. Foreign investment was excluded, or heavily regulated. In Mexico, for example, businesses had to be majority-owned by Mexican nationals. There were restrictions on employing expatriates with needed skills. The business environment was heavily regulated and many industries were state-owned including the oil industry (Pemex) and the telephone system. The political environment, partly for historical reasons, was strongly anti-foreign investment throughout Latin America. Immediately after the Second World War Argentina nationalized the railway system and, when the price of oil was high in the 1970s, Venezuela took over much of the oil industry.

Mexico had nationalistic economic policies in the core of the country but in the north, along the border with the US, it was different. In the Second World War, with labour in short supply in the US, the *bracero* programme was introduced to encourage Mexican workers to come north of the border. The *bracero* programme ceased in the 1960s and Mexico introduced the border industries programme in 1964, with the help of the US. The programme allowed foreign investment in factories (*maquiladoras*) which manufactured for export into US markets. Further, the US applied low tariffs to products entering the American market. Cheap labour was another attraction as was the ability to employ non-Mexican managers and technicians. The programme grew rapidly and long before NAFTA there were thousands of factories on the Mexican side of the border assembling products for the US market and illustrating that foreign investment and export-orientated industrialization could play a role in economic diversification. Clearly Mexico would benefit from more opening up to foreign investment. However, Mexico, having loosened the nationalistic economic policies that had shielded it from some forces, was now drawn into 'the vortex of dynamic interaction' created by more economically advanced states.[14]

When Mexico joined NAFTA in 1993, the value of the peso rose. Foreign companies were building new plants and investment funds were buying shares on the Mexico City stock exchange, particularly in privatized companies like Telemex. As currency flowed in, the peso became overvalued. In 1994 Mexican nationals took the opportunity to change pesos into dollars and currency speculators sold the peso short and drove down its value. The sequence had been: inflow of foreign investment, appreciation in value of the local currency until it was overvalued, followed by a currency crisis and then an economic crisis in which businesses failed and jobs were lost. Subsequently the Mexican economy rebounded but dislocation had occurred as a result of the currency crisis.

Starting in July 1997 the pattern was repeated in Thailand, Indonesia, Malaysia, the Philippines, Hong Kong and South Korea. The currency crisis started in Thailand and quickly spread to the other countries of southeast Asia as investors, fund managers and banks took money out of the region and speculators helped drive down the value of currencies. There was widespread economic dislocation. Businesses closed, economic growth ceased, unemployment rose, poverty increased, living standards fell.[15]

In Hong Kong the government could call on sufficient resources to sustain the value of the Hong Kong dollar and when prices on the Hong Kong stockmarket plunged, as a result of panic selling, the government entered the market and bought up shares.

The Asian episodes illustrated that financial markets do not tend towards equilibrium but are inherently unstable.[16] The instability can dislocate economies and produce widespread social dislocation. Many formerly less developed countries have benefited from opening up national space to outside investment in manufacturing activities that utilize local labour to produce low-cost goods for sale in richer markets, but the inflow and outflow of foreign capital can cause instability. Policy-makers in the US tend to assume that opening economies to the stiff breezes of competition will be bracing and problems will be self-correcting. This view may well be applicable to the US at the present time. The US has such a large economy that it can absorb and dampen corrective forces. The US is a huge importer of goods, industrial raw materials and agricultural commodities. The negative balance of trade exceeded $200 billion in 2000. To set against this deficit is the fact that US corporations have large profitable investments overseas and many foreigners, when they come into possession of US dollars, invest in US stocks, Treasury bonds, real estate, manufacturing plant or service industry outlets. The US is not only the biggest market to sell goods into, it is also the largest economy into which international investment funds are placed. Only a very large economy with the ability to attract and absorb foreign investment is in a position to run a substantial, continuing trade deficit.

Keynes,[17] examining the smaller economy of the UK, came to the conclusion that the UK could not obtain the status of a pure free-trade economy. In a situation of complete free trade Britain would not be able to absorb the deficit on the external trade account, nor would the government be able to exercise control over the economy and provide conditions in which vital growth industries could be nurtured. In these terms it will be difficult for developing countries to produce stable economic conditions in a world without economic borders.

The pace of industrialization, since the Second World War, in the smaller countries on the margins of East Asia has been rapid. Hong Kong, before the Second World War, was primarily a trading and commercial centre. After the war it resumed that function, and unstable conditions in China resulted in migrants seeking refuge in Hong Kong. The result was a large pool of people, many possessing skills and education, that could be used to organize the assembly and distribution of products sold in overseas markets. Labour costs were low, prices of products were competitive, exports grew.

After the communist victory in the Chinese civil war, Taiwan became the home of the defeated nationalist army and many others who thought it best to leave China with the assets they could carry or transfer before the communists sealed off the mainland. Under threat of invasion, and with US help, Taiwan began to develop defence industries on the island. By the late 1960s many products like radio equipment, TV sets and tape recorders were being assembled in Taiwan for sale in US markets. In the 1980s large corporations, manufacturing in Taiwan, were supplying the markets of Europe and North America with VCRs, TVs, compact disc players and video cameras at prices that could not be matched by producers in older industrialized economies. Manufacturing activities involving assembly of many parts, and thus a high labour component, ceased to be viable in economically advanced countries. The process of diffusing manufacturing into regions with low-cost, trainable, disciplined labour forces has proceeded rapidly and some countries including Taiwan and South Korea now make products such as computers and motor cars for markets in North America and Europe.

The transfer of manufacturing activities into regions of low labour costs would not have been achieved so rapidly without major advances in transport and communication technology. The speed and size of vessels increased rapidly after the Second World War. The cost of transporting people and goods by air dropped markedly. Just as important were innovations in the handling of goods. Before the Second World War it was not uncommon for goods to be moved from producer to dockside warehouse and then be loaded by dockers into the holds of vessels prior to the sea voyage, followed by more labour-intensive unloading, at the other end, as goods were placed in rail freight cars or trucks for movement to the warehouses of distributors. There were goods awaiting shipment, goods in transit and goods in warehouses awaiting distribution. Containerization streamlined the system. Producers put goods into containers which moved quickly by road or rail to the dockside to be directly hoisted on to container ships that were, at the end of the voyage, promptly unloaded. It was no longer necessary to have capital tied up in the supply pipeline.

Cheap telephone systems, faxes and e-mails allowed suppliers to respond promptly to the needs of manufacturers and distributors. The cost of shipping dropped and this was comple-mented by the speeding up of the whole process which saved money and allowed distant producers to respond quickly to market forces in Europe and North America.

The evolution of transport and communication technology has been a long process spanning the last two centuries. The recent advances have come rapidly but they are built on a his-tory of technological development that goes back into the nineteenth century. The story so far has been told in Hugill's *Global Communications since 1844: Geopolitics and Technology*.[18]

We have to avoid speaking of economic miracles in Europe[19] or Asia. The so-called four tigers of the Pacific Rim – Singapore, Hong Kong, Taiwan and South Korea – are the result of a long period of investment and infrastructure devel-opment. Singapore was established as a trading and commercial centre by the East India Company in 1819. It had a successful history as an entrepôt and financial centre when the manufac-turing sector expanded rapidly in the 1960s. Hong Kong (1841) was founded specifically as a south China trade and financial centre that developed educated classes of businessmen, entre-preneurs and administrators. Taiwan became a Japanese colony in 1895 and was developed as a source of cane sugar, tropical fruits and minerals. Under Japanese administration, funds were invested in infrastructure – roads, railways, ports, harbours and telecommunications. In general, the population was better edu-cated than in mainland China. Similarly in Korea, which Japan used as a source of minerals and foodstuffs, investments were made in roads, railways and ports that linked the interior of the Korean peninsula to the economy of Japan. Ceasing to be colonies made the tigers more attractive to a greater range of investors but physical infrastructure, education systems and the entrepreneurial classes, established in the colonial era, did not disappear at independence.

China was late to enter the ranks of low-cost-labour countries assembling goods for affluent markets but now is a source of tex-tiles, clothing, household equipment and electronic products for North America and Europe. Other Asian countries that supply advanced markets are Pakistan, India, Bangladesh, Thailand and Indonesia. The conditions in which goods are assembled causes concern. Working conditions are usually poor, and health and safety safeguards not in place. Multinational corporations, which sell, for example, footwear or soccer balls made in Asia on worldwide markets, usually do not own the factories producing the goods but contract with a local entrepreneur to supply the merchandise. Cheap labour has enabled countries to diversify economically but most of the battles concerning workplace conditions still have to be fought. Many see aspects of globalization as a threat, disturbing traditional lifestyles, but failing to produce rising living standards. When the World Trade Organization meets delegates are likely to be picketed by protestors who see globalization as a process that is exploiting the poor of the world and threatening global environments as rain forests are chopped down to provide the raw materials for cheap furniture and timber products assembled in southeast Asia.

Globalization is not simply about opening the world to the free flow of capital, goods and technology, using neoliberal trade policies. Nineteenth-century liberals were in the forefront of battles to abolish slavery, restrict child labour, reform prisons and establish safe working conditions in the Western world. Many of the victories won in the past have now been outflanked by moving manufacturing activities to unregulated regions where citizens have few rights and limited ability to protect themselves against exploitation. Here we approach a central problem with the whole concept of globalization. Globalization is a Western concept – an Anglo-Dutch-American concept that has emerged from the maritime trading world. Free trade is but one of a number of freedoms which include freedom of speech, freedom of religion, a free press, the right to free assembly and a right to dissent. These values are not shared in several areas of the world in which we seek to promote trade. It is easy to say that freedom of expression is a matter for other cultures, or countries, to decide. But just as we try to influence them, they exert pressures upon us. When the President of China made a state visit to Britain in 1999 demonstrators in London, displaying banners protesting the treatment of Tibet, were wrongfully detained, without charge by the police. The banners were torn down by the police. All to avoid giving offence to the leader of a country perceived to be an important trade partner.

Which brings us to the *Clash of Civilizations*.[20] With the diffusion of some popular cultural traits including foodways and clothing styles around the world it is tempting to think that all cultures are becoming more alike. But cultures have deeply rooted institutions and while young people want to experiment with food, dress and music styles it is not so easy to change judicial systems, religious beliefs and the hierarchies of society. Cultures resist change. A good example is Iran. In the late nineteenth century many educated Iranians wanted to adopt Western ways in an effort to modernize the country. The effort gathered pace after 1921 when a military officer took control of the country and proclaimed himself Shah. Modernization continued with the Shah and his son until 1979, when the country erupted against the ruling regime and reverted to an order dominated by Shiite priests and Islamic law. The Middle East, with a strong Islamic heritage, will embrace aspects of modernization but resist Westernization.

China has traditionally been a closed society and has tried to prevent commercial penetration by the West since the late eighteenth century. When weak, the country was unable to resist the establishment of treaty ports, administered by great powers who employed their own legal systems. Most of the Western outposts, at cities like Canton and Shanghai, were suppressed after the communist takeover when the country reverted to being a closed society.

Since the economic reforms of the 1980s it is clear that China wants export-led industrialization. Whether or not foreign businesses can be freely established and run in China on equal terms with indigenous activities is an issue that has not been fully tested. The Chinese legal system is difficult to understand. In Western countries laws are codified and, in theory, equally applied. In China there is a Confucian tradition of examining each case as a special case, while under communist rule many regulations have simply been enforced at the work-unit level. There are few appeal mechanisms.

Japan was forced open to outside commerce by Commander Perry's expedition of 1853. Quickly the Japanese learnt to play the industrialization, modernization, export-driven economy game. In spite of recent recessions Japan will continue to play a major role in the world economy.

India, like Japan, has a version of democracy and a legal code that outsiders can understand. Increasingly India will be a part of the world economy but the continuing hostility between the country and Pakistan might result in a war that has impacts far beyond the subcontinent.

Perhaps Russia is in the process of opening up her economy to the forces of globalization. Certainly the country has the natural resources and assets to form the basis of a major economy within a global system. On the other hand there are parallels between the Russia of today and the country in 1918. An empire has been lost, central government struggles with independence movements in outlying regions, and the economy has not stabilized. The fear is that in economic distress the country will revert to an autarkic system under the control of a dictatorial regime.

Tropical Africa is in economic disarray and torn by conflicts. Many countries lack an effective national government, and countries such as Sierra Leone, Liberia and the Congo are in danger of falling into pieces. However, as tropical Africa is not a major part of the global economic system the failure of countries in the region will have little impact on economic globalization.

In the optimistic scenario NAFTA both embraces South America and creates free trade links with the European Community. Russia stabilizes and expands economically. China continues economic expansion and starts to loosen the political restraints. Japan comes out of recession, and expansion provides stimuli for economic growth on the Pacific Rim. The Middle East continues to receive oil revenues in sufficient quantities to improve living and education standards, which in turn leads to a greater tolerance of non-Islamic cultures. In India the green revolution and the expansion of information-age industries permit living standards to rise and the remnants of the caste society to dissolve. India, with a heritage of democracy, the rule of law and the use of English (the emerging global lingua franca) in the education system, takes its place as a global leader well suited to promote understanding between the world's major culture realms.

There are three major engines in the world economy – Europe, North America and Japan. Of the three, North America is the largest and under US leadership the strongest force for the opening of borders to increased international trade. It is salutary to remember how quickly the roaring '20s with new growth industries such as radio, cinema, consumer goods, automobiles and planes crashed at the end of the decade and how the US, under Smoot-Hawley, led the world into a sustained trade depression in which the forces of globalization fell back, amidst high unemployment and economic dislocation. In the dislocation dictators, with geopolitical policies, advanced the world to war. Why the US intensified protectionism is difficult to understand, for in 1929 the US had trade surpluses with Britain, Canada, France, Germany and Mexico. An exception was Japan but the deficit with Japan did not amount to half the surplus generated by trade with Britain.[21]

It would be a global recession that would lead to geopolitics rising from the deathbed. Countries would follow each other into protectionism and the move towards self-sufficiency would start again. The world would divide into protected trade blocs – North America, South America, Europe, Russia, China and India. Southeast Asian countries would have to opt for arrangements with Japan, China or India.

With policies of self-sufficiency would come the desire to obtain additional territory that contained resources. The world would recreate the patterns of the 1930s but with the Middle East, India and China being more powerful players than they were then.

The geopolitical faultlines still lie around Mackinder's Heartland. The most strategic of the faultlines divides Russia from the new, or re-established, states of Eastern Europe – the Baltics, Belarus, the Ukraine. The faultline has moved to the east but it is still the interface between Russia and East Europe. The states that lie in the lands between the Baltic and Black Seas are a new Middle Tier, which may be vulnerable as Poland and Czechoslovakia were in the first decades of their existence.

In Central Asia the geopolitical faultline has retreated to a nineteenth-century position as the Khanates have reappeared as independent states like Kazakhstan, which have huge oil reserves and the problems of landlocked states trying to get their exports to the sea. The Central Asian states need to avoid dependence on Russia for chaos or imperial resurgence may disrupt the flow of oil. However, the land route to the Persian Gulf is difficult and the Gulf region unstable. Iraq, Iran and Saudi Arabia have all made claims on the Arabian shores of the Gulf. Most of the territory is occupied by sheikdoms that became *de facto* independent in 1899 when they made defence agreements with Britain. Today the sheikdoms are all small, wealthy, independent states that possess large oilfields and armies of migrant workers who feel exploited. Already Iraq has invaded Kuwait, and Iran insists it has claims on islands lying off the Arabian peninsula. Saudi Arabia has made claims on Oman and Bahrein. The Persian Gulf has been given to instability for decades. If the region falls into war and oil exports fail, it could cause a world recession.

In the Far East there are territorial disputes in the South China Sea, a maritime routeway of importance to all countries on the Pacific Rim.[22] China has claims on the Spratly islands, as does Vietnam. Russia and Japan have fought each other several times in the last century (1904, 1939, 1945). At the end of the Second World War the Soviet Union took Sakhalin territory and the Kuril islands from Japan, in the process extending territorial waters and restricting those of Japan. No satisfactory progress has been made towards negotiating the end to this dispute which is a relic of the last weeks of the Second World War. The Pacific Rim geopolitical faultline almost parallels the tectonic fault system as it runs from the Kurils and Sakhalin island to the divided peninsula of Korea, through the Taiwan strait to the South China Sea and the Indonesian archipelago, where the state is threatening to disintegrate into island pieces.

The history of geopolitics is a history of bad ideas – sometimes mad ideas – that have led countries to wars and recessions.

Geopolitik is a German term and Germany has been particularly prone to invest in bad, expansionist policies on more than one front at a time. For Germany the First World War was a crusade to gain resources at the expense of France, control of East Europe at the expense of Russia and colonies at the expense of France, Britain and Belgium. All at a time when Hamburg was established as a leading centre of world trade and Germany could trade easily into the British empire and not incur the costs of running an empire.[23]

Hitler's top priority was not overseas colonies but *Lebensraum* in the east, an idea imbedded in a folk history that drew on fables of medieval Teutonic knights fighting their way into the Slav lands. The fables fuelled faulty thinking. The assumptions behind operation Barbarossa were deadly. It was thought that after the first wave of victories in the west, the Soviet Union would collapse or sue for peace. The *Wehrmacht* did annihilate the Red Army in the west but as it approached the outskirts of Moscow, early in December 1941, there were no fresh forces to be brought into the battle against Marshall Zhukov's experienced Siberian troops brought in from the east. Most senior German officers with logistical understanding had feared this outcome but their views were ignored.

It is true that the Nazi leadership pushed aside informed military opinion in pursuit of slogans, *Lebensraum* and racial exterminations. However, listening to military opinion does not guard against wars you cannot win. In the 1930s the Japanese military started the wars in Manchuria and at the Marco Polo bridge. The same interest group argued for the takeover of Southeast Asia, even though leaders such as Admiral Yamamoto understood that, in a long war, Japan did not have the military capacity to defeat the US.

It is fashionable to argue that such things could not happen in a democracy where a spectrum of interest groups would create a balance and avoid extreme policies. But democracies can fail too. After the crash of 1929 the position of the financial sector was weakened politically and it was unable to stop the passage of the protectionist Smoot-Hawley bill, being pushed by labour and manufacturing interests,[24] at a time when the US had a positive trade balance. As a result of US protectionism world trade collapsed, employment declined in all exporting countries, the hands of those who wanted autarky were strengthened, the number of dictators increased, the road to the Second World War was shortened. And as the signposts on the road became clear the US produced another policy from its geopolitical past – isolation. As George Washington put it in his *Farewell Address*, 'there can be no greater error than to expect or calculate upon real favors between nations.'

References

INTRODUCTION

1 Mark Bassin, 'Friedrich Ratzel 1844–1904', *Geographers Biobibliographical Studies*, XI (1987), pp. 123–32.

2 Some definitions of geopolitics see the subject as the political geography of international relations: David Newman, 'Geopolitics Renaissant: Territory, Sovereignty and the World Political Map', *Geopolitics*, III/1 (1998), p. 1; Klaus Dodds, *Geopolitics in a Changing World* (Harlow, 2000), p. 31, reproduces Kjellén's original definition of geopolitics 'the science which conceives of the state as a geographical organism or as a phenomenon in space' and an inclusive, modern view of the subject as intellectual terrain in which 'geography, knowledge, power and political and social institutions' interact. See also John Agnew, *Geopolitics: Re-visioning World Politics* (London, 1998), pp. 2–3; Jeremy Black, *Maps and Politics* (London, 1997), pp. 110–13.

3 Peter J. Taylor, *The Way the Modern World Works: World Hegemony to World Impasse* (Chichester, 1996), pp. 59–63.

4 J. R. Seeley, *The Expansion of England* (London, 1883), pp. 300–301.

5 H. W. Koch, 'Social Darwinism as a Factor in the New Imperialism', in H. W. Koch, *The Origins of the First World War* (London, 1984), pp. 319–42.

6 John O'Loughlin and Herman van der Wusten, 'Political Geography of Panregions', *The Geographical Review*, LXXX/1 (1990), pp. 1–20.

7 H. J. Mackinder, 'The Geographical Pivot of History', *The Geographical Journal*, XXIII/4, 1904, pp. 421–4; B. W. Blouet, *Halford Mackinder: A Biography* (College Station, TX, 1987), pp. 108–22; Gearóid Ó. Tuathal, *Critical Geopolitics: The Politics of Writing Global Space* (London, 1996), pp. 25–34; W. H. Parker, *Mackinder: Geography as an Aid to Statecraft* (Oxford, 1982); Paul Coones, *Mackinder's 'Scope and Methods of Geography' After a Hundred Years* (Oxford, 1987).

8 James Kurth, 'The Decline and Fall of Almost Everything', *Foreign Affairs*, LXXII/2 (1993), p. 159.

9 Zbigniew Brzezinski, 'The Cold War and its Aftermath', *Foreign Affairs*, LXXI/4 (1992), pp. 31–49; *The Grand Chessboard* (New York, 1997), pp. 34–5.

10 Peter J. Hugill, *Global Communications since 1844: Geopolitics and Technology* (Baltimore, 1999).

11 George Orwell, *Nineteen Eighty Four* (London, 1949).
12 Mackinder, 'The Pivot', p. 436.
13 Geir Lundestad, '*Empire' by Integration: The United States and European Integration, 1945–1997* (Oxford, 1998), p. 8.
14 Martin W. Lewis and Kären E. Wigen, *The Myth of Continents* (Berkeley, CA, 1997).
15 Samuel P. Huntington, *The Clash of Civilizations and the Remaking of World Order* (New York, 1996).
16 Chalmers Johnson, *Blowback: The Costs and Consequences of American Empire* (New York, 2000).
17 Ronald Robinson and John Gallagher, 'The Imperialism of Free Trade', *Economic History Review*, Second Series, VI/1 (1953), pp. 1–15; Wm. Roger Louis, 'Introduction', in Robin W. Winks, *Oxford History of the British Empire, Volume V, Historiography* (Oxford, 1999), pp. 39–40.
18 Saul Cohen, 'The Geopolitics of an Evolving World System: From Conflict to Accommodation', in Paul F. Diehl, ed., *A Road Map to War, Territorial Dimensions of International Conflict* (Nashville, TN, 1999), pp. 271–98.
19 Anthony Giddens, *Runaway World: How Globalization is Reshaping Our Lives* (New York, 2000); Allen J. Scott, *Regions and the World Economy: The Coming Shape of Global Production, Competition, and Political Order* (Oxford, 1998).

I IMPERIALISM, GLOBALIZATION, GEOPOLITICS

1 Martin Lynn, 'British Policy, Trade, and Informal Empire in the Mid-Nineteenth Century', in Andrew Porter, ed., *The Oxford History of the British Empire*, vol. III, *The Nineteenth Century* (Oxford, 1999), pp. 101–21. John Gallagher and Ronald Robinson, 'The Imperialism of Free Trade', *Economic History Review*, second series, VI (1953), pp. 1–15.
2 Henry Kissinger, *Diplomacy* (New York, 1994), p. 138.
3 Fernand Braudel, *The Identity of France: Vol. I History and Environment*, trans. from the French by Siân Reynolds (London, 1988), p. 318.
4 Alan Sykes, *Tariff Reform in British Politics, 1903–1913* (Oxford, 1979).
5 Paul Kennedy, *The Rise of the Anglo-German Antagonism 1860–1914* (London, 1987).
6 Donald W. Meinig, *The Shaping of America: A Geographical Perspective on 500 Years of History, Volume II, Continental America 1800–1867* (New Haven, CN, 1993). Meining makes it clear that US expansion was imperial in nature.
7 Carl O. Sauer, 'The Formative Years of Ratzel in the United States', *Annals of the Association of American Geographers*, LXI (1971), pp. 245–54.
8 Frederick Jackson Turner, 'The Significance of the Frontier in American History', in *The Frontier in American History* (New York, 1920).
9 James C. Malin, 'Space and History: Reflections on the Closed-Space Doctrines of Turner and Mackinder and the Challenge to Those Ideas by the Air Age', *Agricultural History*, XVIII (1944), pp. 65–74, 107–26.
10 Alfred Thayer Mahan, *The Influence of Seapower Upon History, 1660–1783*

(Boston, MA, 1890).

11 *Ibid.*, p. 33.

12 *Ibid.*, pp. 27–35.

13 Theodore Roosevelt, *Atlantic Monthly*, LXVI (October 1890), p. 567.

14 Richard W. Turk, *The Ambiguous Relationship: Theodore Roosevelt and Alfred Thayer Mahan* (New York, 1987).

15 A. T. Mahan, *The Problem of Asia and its Effects upon International Policies* (Boston, 1900), p. 4. Brian W. Blouet, 'The Problem of Asia and the World View of Admiral Mahan', in Clive H. Schofield, ed., *Global Boundaries: World Boundaries*, vol. I (London, 1994), pp. 36–9.

16 Mahan, *Asia*, pp. 30–32.

17 *Ibid.*, p. 46.

18 *Ibid.*, p. 98.

19 Alan Sharp, *The Versailles Settlement: Peacemaking in Paris, 1919* (New York, 1991), p. 1.

20 Mahan, *Asia*, p. 120.

21 *Ibid.*, p. 167.

22 *Ibid.*, p. 139.

23 *Ibid.*, p. 191.

24 *Ibid.*, p. 129.

25 *Ibid.*, p. 17.

26 H. J. Mackinder, 'The Geographical Pivot of History', *Geographical Journal*, XXIII/4 (April 1904), pp. 421–44.

27 *Ibid.*, p. 434.

28 H. J. Mackinder, 'Foreword', in N. Mikhaylov, *Soviet Geography: The New Industrial and Economic Distributions of the USSR*, trans. from the Russian by Natalie Rothstein (London, 1937), 2nd edn.

29 Mackinder, 'Pivot', pp. 436–7.

30 W. H. Parker, *Mackinder: Geography as an Aid to Statecraft* (Oxford, 1982).

31 Mackinder, 'Pivot', p. 441.

32 *Ibid.*, p. 438.

33 Mark Bassin, 'Friedrich Ratzel 1844–1904', *Geographers Biobibliographical Studies*, XI (1987), pp. 123–32.

34 F. Ratzel, 'The Territorial Growth of States', *Scottish Geographical Magazine*, XII/7 (July 1896), pp. 351–61.

35 *Ibid.*, p. 355.

36 *Ibid.*, p. 351.

37 Harriet Wanklyn, *Friedrich Ratzel* (Cambridge, 1961).

38 Mark Bassin, 'Imperialism and the Nation State in Friedrich Ratzel's Political Geography', *Progress in Human Geography*, II (1987), pp. 473–95.

39 Woodruff D. Smith, *The Ideological Origins of Nazi Imperialism* (New York, 1986), p. 149.

40 Sven Holdar, 'The Ideal State and the Power of Geography: The Life-Work of Rudolf Kjellén', *Political Geography*, II/2 (1992), pp. 307–23; Bertil Haggman, 'Rudolf Kjellén and Modern Swedish Geopolitics', *Geopolitics*, III/2 (1998), pp. 99–112.

41 Darrell Bates, *The Fashoda Incident of 1898: Encounter on the Nile* (Oxford,

1984), and Susan Peterson, *Crisis Bargaining and the State: The Domestic Politics of International Conflict* (Ann Arbor, 1996), pp. 95–132.

42 G. P. Gooch and Harold Temperley, *British Documents on the Origins of the War: 1898–1914* (London, 1928), pp. 397–420; see also Zara S. Steiner, *Britain and the Origins of the First World War* (New York, 1977), pp. 44–5, 183–5; Richard A. Cosgrove, 'The Career of Sir Eyre Crowe', *Albion*, IV/4, 1972, pp. 193–205.

43 C. J. Barnett, *Defence and Diplomacy: Britain and the Great Powers, 1815–1914* (Manchester, 1993), p. 111.

44 David Thomas Murphy, *The Heroic Earth: Geopolitical Thought in Weimar Germany, 1918–1933* (Kent, OH, 1997).

2 THE GEOPOLITICS OF THE FIRST WORLD WAR, 1914–19

1 Isaiah Bowman, *The New World: Problems in Political Geography* (Yonkers-on-Hudson, NY, 1921), pp. 8–9.

2 David Stevenson, *French War Aims Against Germany 1914–1918* (Oxford, 1982), and Walter A. McDougall, *France's Rhineland Diplomacy 1914–1924: The Lost Bid for a Balance of Power in Europe* (Princeton, NJ, 1978).

3 Dietrich Geyer, *Russian Imperialism* (New Haven, CT, 1987) and Hugh Ragsdale, *Imperial Russian Foreign Policy* (New York, 1993).

4 Niall Ferguson, *The Pity of War* (London, 1998), pp. 161–5; and Bethmann Hollweg, *Reflections on the World War* (London, 1920), pp. 149–52.

5 Viscount Grey of Fallodon, *Twenty-Five Years: 1892–1916* (New York, 1925), vol. II, p. 321; Sir Edward Grey's speech to the House of Commons, 3 August 1914 is at H. C. Debs., 5th ser., vol. LXV, col. 1824, for 'prevent the whole of the West of Europe … falling under the domination of a single power', and David Stevenson, *The First World War and International Politics* (Oxford, 1988), p. 36.

6 The Co-Efficients were founded by Beatrice and Sidney Webb in 1902. The group included Sir Edward Grey, Lord Haldane, a future Minister of War, Bertrand Russell, H. G. Wells, Mackinder, L. S. Amery and several influential journalists. Minutes were printed.

7 C. Jay Smith, Jr, 'Great Britain and the 1914–1915 Straits Agreement with Russia: The British Promise of November 1914', *American Historical Review*, LXX/4 (1965), pp. 1033–4.

8 Thomas Edward La Fargue, *China and the World War* (Stanford, CA, 1937), p. 233; The Twenty-One Demands of 1915, pp. 241–3.

9 Arthur S. Link, ed., *The Papers of Woodrow Wilson* (Princeton, NJ, 1984), vol. 45, p. 13.

10 Fritz Fischer, *Germany's Aims in the First World War* (New York, 1967), pp. 103–5.

11 *Ibid.*, p. 104.

12 Friedrich Naumann, *Mitteleuropa* (Berlin, 1915). Published in translation in London, 1916, and New York, 1917, the book was analysed as a possible basis for a negotiated peace by some commentators.

13 H. C. Debs., 5th ser., vol. LXXVII, col. 1299–1307, 10 January 1916.

14 Paul M. Kennedy, *The Rise of the Anglo-German Antagonism 1860–1914* (London, 1980).
15 Ferguson, *Pity of War*, pp. 286–90.
16 *Ibid.*, p. 438.
17 Link, *Woodrow Wilson*, vol. 45, pp. 468–73; Lawrence Gelfand, *The Inquiry: American Preparations for Peace* (New Haven, CT, 1963). The Inquiry was set up in 1917 to assemble information for peace talks.
18 Link, *Woodrow Wilson*, vol. 45, pp. 534–9.
19 George W. Egerton, *Great Britain and the Creation of the League of Nations: Strategy, Politics, and International Organization, 1914–1919* (Chapel Hill, NC, 1978).
20 'A Compilation of the Messages and Papers of the Presidents' (New York, 1925), vol. XVII, pp. 8532–5; Link, *Woodrow Wilson*, vol. 48, pp. 514–17.
21 Link, *Woodrow Wilson*, vol. 49, pp. 415–16.
22 Victor Rothwell, *British War Aims and Peace Diplomacy 1914–1918* (Oxford, 1971), pp. 30–32; David French, *The Strategy of the Lloyd George Coalition 1916–1918* (Oxford, 1995); Erik Goldstein, *Winning the Peace* (Oxford, 1991).
23 Hugh Seton-Watson and Christopher Seton-Watson, *The Making of a New Europe: R.W. Seton-Watson and the Last Years of Austria-Hungary* (London, 1981).
24 Ferguson, *Pity of War*, pp. 440–41.
25 Robert Lansing, *The Peace Negotiations: A Personal Narrative* (Boston and New York, 1921), pp. 97–101.

3 WHO RULES EAST EUROPE COMMANDS THE HEARTLAND

1 John Barnes and David Nicholson, *The Leo Amery Diaries, Volume 1, 1896–1929* (London, 1980), Entry, 24 March 1919.
2 Alan Sharp, *The Versailles Settlement: Peacemaking in Paris, 1919* (New York, 1991), p. 31.
3 *Ibid.*, p. 120.
4 Robert Lansing, *The Peace Negotiations: A Personal Narrative* (Boston and New York, 1921), p. 37.
5 H. J. Mackinder, *Democratic Ideals and Reality: A Study in the Politics of Reconstruction* (London, 1919).
6 *Ibid.*, p.141.
7 *Ibid.*, p.194.
8 *Ibid.*, p.205.
9 *Ibid.*, p.35.
10 Brian W. Blouet, *Halford Mackinder: A Biography* (College Station, TX, 1987), pp. 170–71.
11 Albert Demangeon, *Le déclin de l'Europe* (Paris, 1920); *America and the Race for World Domination* (Garden City, NY, 1921), page numbers refer to the latter; Geoffrey Parker, 'Albert Demangeon' in T. W. Freeman, *Geographers Biobibliographical Studies* (London, 1987), II, pp. 13–21; Geoffrey Parker, 'French Geopolitical Thought in the Inter-war Years

and the Emergence of the European Idea,' *Political Geography Quarterly*,
VI (1987), pp. 145–50.
12 Demangeon, *ibid.*, pp. 16–17.
13 *Ibid.*, pp. 29–31.
14 *Ibid.*, p. 38.
15 *Ibid.*, p. 52.
16 *Ibid.*, chap. 7.
17 *Ibid.*, p. 197, p. 107.
18 Geoffrey Parker, *Geopolitics* (London, 1998), p. 51.
19 Geoffrey J. Martin, *The Life and Thought of Isaiah Bowman* (Hamden, CT, 1980).
20 Isaiah Bowman, *The New World: Problems in Political Geography* (Yonkers-on-Hudson, NY, 1921).
21 *Ibid.*, p. 5; Michael Burns, 'Disturbed Spirits: Minority Rights and New World Orders, 1919 and the 1990s', in Samuel F. Wells, Jr and Paula Bailey Smith, *New European Orders, 1919 and 1991* (Washington, DC, 1996), pp. 41–61.
22 *Ibid.*, p. 3.
23 *Ibid.*, p. 8; Martin, op. cit., p. 97.
24 *Ibid.*, pp. 86–9.
25 *Ibid.*, pp. 193–5, p. 203.
26 *Ibid.*, p. 242.
27 *Ibid.*, pp. 253–7.
28 *Ibid.*, p. 351.
29 Neil Smith, 'Bowman's New World and the Council on Foreign Relations', *Geographical Review*, LXXVI (1986), pp. 438–60.
30 Holger H. Herwig, 'Geopolitik: Haushofer, Hitler and Lebensraum', in Colin S. Gray and Geoffrey Sloan, eds, *Geopolitics, Geography and Strategy* (London, 1999), pp. 218–41; Henning Heske, 'Karl Haushofer: His Role in German Geopolitics and in Nazi Politics', *Political Geography Quarterly*, VI (1987), pp. 135–44; Henning Heske and Rolf Wesche, 'Karl Haushofer 1869–1946', *Geographers: Biobibliographical Studies*, XII (1988), pp. 95–106.
31 Daniel Deudney, 'Geopolitics and Change', in Michael W. Doyle and G. John Ikenberry, eds, *New Thinking in International Relations Theory* (Boulder, CO, 1997), pp. 91–123; Mark Bassin, 'Race Contra Space: the Conflict between German *Geopolitik* and National Socialism', *Political Geography Quarterly*, VI (1987), pp. 134–55.
32 Guntram Henrik Herb, *Under the Map of Germany: Nationalism and Propaganda, 1918–1945* (London, 1997).
33 Geoffrey Parker, *Western Geopolitical Thought in the Twentieth Century* (New York, 1985).
34 Herwig, 'Geopolitik', p. 224; Robert E. Dickinson, *The German Lebensraum* (New York, 1943).
35 Geoffrey Stoakes, *Hitler and the Quest for World Domination* (Leamington Spa, 1986), p. 153.
36 *Ibid.*, p. 149.
37 Parker, *Western Geopolitical*, pp. 65–9.

38 Peter J. Hugill, *Global Communications since 1844: Geopolitics and Technology* (Baltimore, MD, 1999), pp. 5–7. See also Richard Rosecrance, 'The Commercial Society and International Relations', in Eugene D. Genovese and Leonard Hochberg, eds, *Geographic Perspectives in History* (Oxford, 1989), and Edward Whiting Fox, *History in Geographic Perspective: The Other France* (New York, 1971).

39 Eberhard Jäckel, *Hitler's World View: A Blueprint for Power* (Cambridge, MA, 1981).

40 Gearóid Ó Tuathail, Simon Dalby and Paul Routledge, eds, *The Geopolitics Reader* (London, 1998), p. 39.

41 John W. Wheeler-Bennett, 'The Meaning of Brest-Litovsk Today', *Foreign Affairs*, 17, 1938, p. 152.

42 Alan Bullock, *Hitler and Stalin; Parallel Lives* (London, 1998), 2nd edn.

43 Herwig, *Geopolitik*, p. 227, fig. 2.

44 John O'Louglin and Herman van der Wursten, 'Political Geography of Panregions', *Geographical Review*, LXXX (1990), pp. 1–20.

45 F. W. Winterbotham, *The Nazi Connection* (New York, 1978), pp. 53–4.

46 Herwig, *Geopolitik*, pp. 225–6.

47 Stoakes, *World Domination*, pp. 54–5; Mark Bassin, 'Race Contra Space: The Conflict between German Geopolitik and National Socialism', *Political Geography Quarterly*, VI/2 (1987), pp. 115–34.

48 Tuathail, *Reader*, p. 36.

49 Heske and Wesche, *Karl Haushofer*, p. 96.

50 Herwig, *Geopolitik*, pp. 232–3.

51 *Ibid.*, pp. 230–31.

52 Edmund Walsh, *Total Power: A Footnote to History* (New York, 1948).

53 William H. Honan, *Visions of Infamy* (New York, 1991), pp. 27–9.

54 Hector C. Bywater, *Sea Power in the Pacific: A Study of the American-Japanese Naval Problem* (London, 1921), p. 254; on naval intelligence, Hector C. Bywater and H. C. Ferraby, *Strange Intelligence: Memoirs of Naval Secret Service* (London, 1931), and Hector C. Bywater, *Their Secret Purposes: Dramas and Mysteries of the Naval War* (London, 1932). Bywater also published a novel, *The Great Pacific War: A History of the American-Japanese Campaign 1931–33* (London, 1925).

55 Bywater, *Sea Power in the Pacific*, pp. 255–7.

56 *Ibid.*, p. 287.

57 *Ibid.*, p. 280.

58 *Ibid.*, p. 271.

59 Honan, *Visions of Infamy*, p. 67.

60 Paolo E. Coletta, ed, *American Secretaries of the Navy* (Annapolis, MD, 1980), II (1913–72), p. 586.

61 Count Heinrich Coudenhove-Kalergi, *Anti-Semitism Throughout the Ages* (London, 1935). This is a new edition edited and updated by Count Richard.

62 Count Richard Coudenhove-Kalergi, *Pan Europe* (New York, 1926), p. 22, originally published 1923.

63 *Ibid.*, pp. 4–8.

64 *Ibid.*, p. 55.

65 *Ibid.*, pp. 20–21.

66 *Ibid.*, p. 45.

67 *Ibid.*, p.132.

68 *Ibid.*, pp. 36–42; Derek Heater, *The Idea of European Unity* (New York, 1992), p. 126, shows a map of Coudenhove-Kalergi's world view.

69 Barnes and Nicholson, op. cit., p. 477; L. S. Amery, *My Political Life: Volume Three: The Unforgiving Years 1929–1940* (London, 1955), pp. 44–7; Martin Gilbert, *'Never Despair' Winston S. Churchill 1945–1965* (London, 1988), p. 243. See *Who Was Who 1971–1980* (New York, 1981), p. 175; R. N. Coudenhove-Kalergi, *An Idea Conquers the World* (London, 1953); and Richard N. Coudenhove-Kalergi, *Crusade for Pan-Europe: Autobiography of a Man and a Movement* (New York, 1943), for more on the life of the Count.

70 Count Richard N. Coudenhove-Kalergi, *The Totalitarian State Against Man* (London, 1938).

71 *Ibid.*, pp. 114–18. Wickham Stead wrote an introduction to *The Totalitarian State* and indicates he does disapprove of Mussolini's policies.

72 *Ibid.*, p. 89.

73 Edith Wynner and Georgia Lloyd, *Searchlight on Peace Plans: Choose Your Road to World Government* (New York, 1944); Derek Heater, *The Idea of European Unity* (New York, 1992).

74 L. S. Amery, *My Political Life: Volume Three*, pp. 46–7.

75 Andrea Bosco, 'Lord Lothian and the Federalist Critique of National Sovereignty,' in David Long and Peter Wilson, eds, *Thinkers of the Twenty Year Crisis* (Oxford, 1995), pp. 247–76.

76 Roger Berthoud, 'The Idealist who sold Churchill to the World', *The Times*, 7 September 1981, p. 8; Martin Gilbert, ed., *Winston Churchill and Emery Reves Correspondence 1937–1964* (Austin, TX, 1997).

4 THE COLLAPSE OF WORLD ORDER

1 D. J. Markwell, 'J. M. Keynes, Idealism and the Economic Bases of Peace', in David Long and Peter Wilson, eds, *Thinkers of the Twenty Year Crisis: Inter-War Idealism Reassessed* (Oxford, 1995), pp. 190–91.

2 Adam Fergusson, *When Money Dies: The Nightmare of the Weimar Collapse* (London, 1975).

3 Ideas concerning autarky were widely diffused in the 1930s. Even Keynes (see 1 above) wrote on national self-sufficiency. Nationalist economic ideas were adopted by Mexico, after the revolution, and Brazil (Estado Nôvo) in the 1930s. The theory of the import substitution policy adopted in Latin America after the Second World War can be traced to Central European economic theory of the 1920s.

4 Wilhelm Deist, Manfred Messerschmidt, Hans-Erich Volkmann and Wolfram Wette, *Germany and the Second World War: Volume I, The Build-up of German Aggression* (Oxford, 1990), vol. I, pp. 173–4.

5 N. J. G. Pounds, *An Historical Geography of Europe* (Cambridge, 1990), p. 428; David J. M. Hooson, *A New Soviet Heartland?* (Princeton, NJ,

1964). W. H. Parker, *An Historical Geography of Russia* (Chicago, 1968).

6 Simon Reich, *Fruits of Fascism: Postwar Prosperity in Historical Perspective* (Ithaca, NY, 1990), pp. 294–5.

7 David Atkinson, 'Geopolitics, Cartography and Geographical Knowledge: Envisioning Africa from Fascist Italy', in Morag Bell, Robin Butlin and Michael Heffernan, eds, *Geography and Imperialism* (Manchester, 1995), pp. 265–97.

8 Norman Rich, *Hitler's War Aims: Ideology, the Nazi State, and the Course of Expansion* (New York, 1992), p. 86.

9 Elizabeth Wiskemann, 'Czechs and Germans after Munich', *Foreign Affairs*, XVII, 1939, p. 301.

10 Walter Lippmann, *The Communist World and Ours* (Boston, 1959), p. 17.

11 Henry Kissinger, 'Stalin's Bazaar', in *Diplomacy*; George F. Kennan, *Soviet Foreign Policy 1917–1941* (Princeton, NJ, 1960), pp. 90–102; Igor Lukes, *Czechoslovakia between Hitler and Stalin* (New York, 1996), p. 258.

12 H. R. Trevor-Roper, ed., *Blitzkrieg to Defeat: Hitler's War Directives 1939–1945* (New York, 1964), pp. 49–52.

13 Richard Overy, *Russia's War* (London, 1997), pp. 61–2.

14 John Charmley, *Churchill: The End of Glory* (London, 1993).

15 John W. Wheeler-Bennett, *King George VI: His Life and Reign* (New York, 1958), pp. 390–92.

16 George McJimsey, *The Presidency of Franklin Delano Roosevelt* (Lawrence, KS, 2000), pp. 185–214.

17 *The Public Papers and Addresses of Franklin D. Roosevelt, 1939 Volume: War and Neutrality* (London, 1941), pp. 185–6.

18 *Ibid.*, pp. 189–90; Patrick J. Hearden, *Roosevelt Confronts Hitler: America's Entry into World War II* (Dekalb, IL, 1987).

19 F. H. Hinsley, *Hitler's Strategy* (Cambridge, 1951). *The Public Papers and Addresses of Franklin D. Roosevelt, 1940 Volume: War and Aid to Democracies* (London, 1941), pp. 198–201, 16 May 1940; Norman J. W. Goda, *Tomorrow the World: Hitler, Northwest Africa, and the Path Toward America* (College Station, TX, 1998); Randall L. Schweller, *Deadly Imbalances: Tripolarity and Hitler's Strategy of World Conquest* (New York, 1998), p. 101.

20 *Roosevelt*, pp. 633–44.

21 Ross T. McIntire, *White House Physician* (New York, 1946), pp. 119–20. See also Robert A. Divine, *Roosevelt and World War II* (New York, 1970).

5 THE NEW ORDER OF 1942

1 Alan S. Milward, *The Fascist Economy of Norway* (Oxford, 1972), p. 3; R. J. Overy, *War and Economy in the Third Reich* (Oxford, 1994), p. 22.

2 Wilhelm Deist, Manfred Messerschmidt, Hans-Erich Volkmann and Wolfram Wette, *Germany and the Second World War: Volume I, The Build-up of German Aggression* (Oxford, 1990), p. 351, pp. 355–60.

3 Herbert Feis, *The Spanish Story: Franco and the Nations at War* (New York, 1948); Paul Preston, *Franco: A Biography* (New York, 1994).

4 Albert Speer, *Inside the Third Reich* (New York, 1970), p. 319.

5 Vojtech Mastny, *The Czechs under Nazi Rule: The Failure of National Resistence, 1939–1942* (New York, 1971), pp. 63–85.

6 H. R. Trevor-Roper, ed., *Blitzkrieg to Defeat: Hitler's War Directives 1939–1945* (New York, 1964), p. 49.

7 Michael Dynes, 'Hitler Planned US Pact to Isolate Britain', *The Times* (27 November 1993), p. 1.

8 Mark Harrison, *Soviet Planning in Peace and War, 1938–1945* (Cambridge, 1985), p. 64, Table 5.

9 *Ibid.*, p. 78.

10 Mark Harrison, 'The Second World War', in R. W. Davies, Mark Harrison, S. G. Wheatcroft, eds, *The Economic Transformation of the Soviet Union, 1913–1945* (Cambridge, 1994), p. 253.

11 *Ibid.*, p. 243.

12 Albert Speer, *Inside the Third Reich* (New York, 1970), p. 184.

13 *Ibid.*, p. 189.

14 *New York Times* (21 December 1941), p. 31; Harold A. Winters with Gerald E. Galloway, William J. Reynolds and David W. Rhyne, *Battling the Elements: Weather and Terrain in the Conduct of War* (Baltimore, MD, 1998), pp. 86–95; *Effects of Climate on Combat in European Russia* (Washington, DC, 1952).

15 Harrison, 'The Second World War', p. 241; Mark Harrison, *Accounting for War: Soviet Production, Employment and the Defence Burden 1940–1945* (Cambridge, 1996), pp. 12–13.

16 John Erickson, *The Road to Stalingrad* (London, 1985), pp. 72–3; Alan Bullock, *Hitler and Stalin* (New York, 1993), p. 549; David M. Glantz, *Stumbling Colossus: The Red Army on the Eve of World War* (Lawrence, KS, 1998).

17 Nicholas Basseches, 'Is Russia Ready for War?', *The Spectator* (14 July 1939), pp. 43–4.

18 Michael Burleigh, *Germany Turns Eastward* (Cambridge, 1988).

19 Horst Boog et al., *Germany and the Second World War: Volume IV The Attack on the Soviet Union* (Oxford, 1998), pp. 136–9; Robert Cecil, *Hitler's Decision to Invade Russia 1941* (London, 1975).

20 Brian Urquhart, *A Life in Peace and War* (New York, 1987), pp. 71–5.

21 Rolf-Dieter Müller, 'The Failure of the Economic Blitzkrieg Strategy' in Horst Boog et al., *Germany and the Second World War, Volume IV, The Attack on the Soviet Union* (Oxford, 1998), p. 1166; Rolf-Dieter Müller and Gerd R. Uebershär, *Hitler's War in the East, 1941–1945* (Oxford, 1997), pp. 283–314.

22 Alexander Dallin, *German Rule in Russia 1941–1945* (London, 1981), 2nd edn, pp. 378–81.

23 *Ibid.*, p. 407.

24 B. R. Mitchell, *International Historical Statistics: Europe, 1750–1993* (New York, 1998), 4th edn.

25 Werner Warmbrunn, *The Dutch Under German Occupation, 1940–1945* (Stanford, CA, 1963), p. 72.

26 Alan Milward, *The New Order and the French Economy* (Oxford, 1970), p. 257, Table 53.

27 P. Lamartine Yates, *Food Production in Western Europe* (London, 1940);
P. Lamartine Yates and Doreen Warriner, *Food and Farming in Post-War Europe* (Oxford, 1943).

28 M. Livi-Bacci, *Population and Nutrition* (Cambridge, 1990), p. 45.

29 Auraham Barkai, *Nazi Economic Ideology, Theory and Policy* (New Haven, CT, 1990), pp. 234–5.

30 Alan S. Milward, *War, Economy and Society* (Berkeley, CA, 1977), p. 135.

31 Barkai, *Nazi Economic Ideology*, p. 258, Table 10.

32 Mitchell, *International Historical Statistics*, p. 577.

33 Alan Milward, *French Economy*, 1970, p. 283.

34 Robert O. Paxton, *Vichy France: Old Guard and New Order, 1940–1944* (New York, 1972), p. 11.

35 Alexander Werth, *France 1940–1945* (New York, 1956), p. 97.

36 Simon Reich, *The Fruits of Fascism: Postwar Prosperity in Historical Perspective* (Ithaca, NY, 1990), pp. 295–7.

37 Neil Smith in John O'Loughlin, ed., *Dictionary of Geopolitics* (Westport, CT, 1994), p. 30.

38 Isaiah Bowman, *The New World: Problems in Political Geography, Supplement* (Yonkers-on-Hudson, NY, 1923), pp. 54–5.

39 David Flath, *The Japanese Economy* (Oxford, 2000), pp. 46–9.

40 Yoriko Fukushima, 'Japanese Geopolitics and its Background: What is the Real Legacy of the Past', *Political Geography*, XVI (1997), p. 410; Joyce C. Lebra, ed., *Japan's Greater East Asia Co-Prosperity Sphere in World War II: Selected Readings and Documents* (Kuala Lumpur, 1975), p. XIII; Michael A. Barnhart, *Japan Prepares for Total War: The Search for Economic Security* (Ithaca, NY, 1987).

41 W. G. Beasley, *Japanese Imperialism 1894–1945* (Oxford, 1987), pp. 223–8.

42 Peter Liberman, *'Does Conquest Pay?'* (Princeton, NJ, 1996).

43 Mark Harrison, *Accounting for War: Soviet Production, Employment, and the Defence Burden, 1940–1945* (Cambridge, 1996), p. 172.

44 Richard Vinen, *The Politics of French Business* (Cambridge, 1991), pp. 151–6.

45 William Rees-Mogg, 'Is this the Next Adolf?', *The Times* (14 February 2000), p. 16; John Gillingham, *Coal, Steel, and the Rebirth of Europe, 1945–1955* (Cambridge, 1991), pp. 67–72; John Gillingham, *Industry and Politics in the Third Reich: Ruhr Coal, Hitler and Europe* (New York, 1985), pp. 146–51.

6 PLANNING THE POSTWAR WORLD

1 Rt Hon. The Earl of Avon, *The Eden Memoirs: The Reckoning* (London, 1965), pp. 289–94; Robert Rhodes James, *Anthony Eden: A Biography* (New York, 1987), pp. 258–60.

2 John Lewis Gaddis, *The United States and the Origins of the Cold War* (New York, 1972), pp. 13–14; *Foreign Relations of the United States, 1942 vol. III Europe*, pp. 504–12; Louis Fischer, *The Road to Yalta: Soviet Foreign Relations, 1941–1945* (New York, 1972), p. 104.

3   Douglas Brinkley and David R. Facey-Crowther, eds, *The Atlantic Charter* (London, 1994); David Dilks, ed., *The Diaries of Sir Alexander Cadogan 1938–45* (London, 1971), pp. 396–402.
4   Emery Reves, 'The Atlantic Charter and Beyond', *Public Affairs*, VI/3 (1943), pp. 125–9.
5   Emery Reves, *The Democratic Manifesto* (London, 1943), p. 80.
6   *Ibid.*, pp. 101–2; Martin Gilbert, ed., *Winston Churchill and Emery Reves: Correspondence, 1937–1964* (Austin, TX, 1997), p. 15.
7   George F. Kennan, *Russia and the West Under Lenin and Stalin* (Boston, 1960), p. 361.
8   Warren F. Kimball, *Swords or Ploughshares? The Morgenthau Plan for Defeated Nazi Germany, 1943–46* (New York, 1976), pp. 15–16.
9   Charles L. Mee, Jr., *Meeting at Potsdam* (New York, 1975), appendix II, The Potsdam Declaration, XIII, Orderly Transfers of German Populations.
10 Professor Jean Gottmann, personal communication.
11 N. J. Spykman, *America's Strategy in World Politics: The United States and the Balance of Power* (New York, 1942).
12 *Ibid.*, p. 260.
13 *Richmond-Times Dispatch*, 9 July 1942.
14 Joseph J. Thorndike, Jr., 'Geopolitics', *Life*, 21 December 1942, pp. 106–15.
15 *Life*, 11 January 1943, p. 3.
16 N. J. Spykman, *The Geography of the Peace*, ed. Helen R. Nichol (New York, 1944), p. 41.
17 Alexander P. de Seversky, *Victory Through Air Power* (New York, 1942).
18 *Ibid.*, pp. 35–7.
19 *Ibid.*, pp. 87–92.
20 *Ibid.*, pp. 95–8.
21 *Ibid.*, pp. 114–15.
22 *Ibid.*, p. 145.
23 *Ibid.*, Chapter 11.
24 Robert Strausz-Hupé, *Geopolitics: The Struggle for Space and Power* (New York, 1942), IX; Andrew Crampton and Gearóid Ó Tuathal, 'Intellectuals, Institutions and Ideology: The Case of Robert Strausz-Hupé and American Geopolitics', *Political Geography*, XV/6–7, 1996, pp. 533–5. See Gearóid Ó Tuathal, *Critical Geopolitics* (Minneapolis, MN, 1996), pp. 119–25 for discussion of American films with a geopolitical theme.
25 Hans W. Weigert, *Generals and Geographers: The Twilight of Geopolitics* (New York, 1942); Derwent Whittlesey, Charles Colby and Richard Hartshorne, *German Strategy for World Conquest* (New York, 1942); Andrew Gyorgy, *Geopolitics: A New German Science* (Berkeley, CA, 1944), Publications in International Relations, III/3, pp. 141–304.
26 Halford J. Mackinder, *Democratic Ideals and Reality* (New York, 1942); G. Douhet, *Il Dominio del' Aria* (Rome, 1921), translated into English and published as *The Command of the Air* (New York, 1942).
27 *Life*, 14 July 1941, p. 20.
28 Walter Lippmann, 'America's Great Mistake', *Life*, 21 July 1941, pp. 74–80.

29 Walter Lippmann, *US Foreign Policy: Shield of the Republic* (Boston, MA, 1943), p. 135.
30 *Ibid.*, pp. 132–3.
31 *Ibid.*, pp. 146–51.
32 Walter Lippmann, *US War Aims* (Boston, MA, 1944).
33 John Lewis Gaddis, *The United States and the Origins of the Cold War 1941–1947* (New York, 1972), pp. 8–10.
34 Simon Reich, *The Fruits of Fascism: Postwar Prosperity in Historical Perspective* (Ithaca, NY, 1990).
35 Halford J. Mackinder, 'The Round World and the Winning of the Peace', *Foreign Affairs*, XXI (1943), pp. 595–605.
36 Carolyn Woods Eisenberg, *Drawing the Line: The American Decision to Divide Germany, 1944–1949* (Cambridge, 1996).
37 Henry Morgenthau, Jr., *Germany Is Our Problem* (New York, 1945).
38 *The Economist* (23 September 1944), p. 407.
39 K. Sainsbury, *Churchill and Roosevelt at War* (New York, 1994), p. 139.
40 Morgenthau, *Germany Is Our Problem*, 'Program to Prevent, Germany from Starting World War III', p. 1.
41 *Ibid.*, pp. 20–24.
42 Eisenberg, *Drawing the Line*, p. 35.
43 Godfrey Hodgson, *The Colonel: The Life and Wars of Henry Stimson, 1867–1950* (New York, 1990), pp. 264–5.
44 Morgenthau, *Germany Is Our Problem*, pp. 31–44.
45 Irwin M. Wall, *The United States and the Making of Post War France, 1945–1954* (Cambridge, 1991), pp. 188–9.
46 A. W. DePorte, *De Gaulle's Foreign Policy 1944–1946* (Cambridge, MA, 1968).
47 Sumner Welles, *The Time for Decision* (New York, 1944).

7 THE COLD WAR AND THE TRIUMPH OF GEOPOLITICS

1 David Held, Anthony McGrew, David Goldblatt and Jonathan Perration, *Global Transformations* (Oxford, 2000), p. 425.
2 S. Siebel-Achenbeck, *Lower Silesia from Nazi Germany to Communist Poland, 1942–49* (New York, 1994), p. 121.
3 Elizabeth Wiskemann, *Germany's Eastern Neighbours* (London, 1956), p. 95.
4 G. Gardiner, 'Czechs and Germans', *New Statesman and Nation* (11 August 1945) and 'Migration of Death', *The Spectator* (26 October 1945).
5 Norman J. G. Pounds, *Eastern Europe* (Chicago, 1969), pp. 62–6.
6 P. R. Magocsi, *Historical Atlas of East Central Europe* (Seattle, WA, 1993), maps 44 and 47. Walter Fitzgerald, *The New Europe* (Westport, CT, 1980), originally published 1946.
7 K. Hitchens, *Rumania 1866–1947* (Oxford, 1994), p. 446.
8 H. N. Brailsford, 'Frontiers and Migrants', *The New Statesman and Nation* (13 January 1945), pp. 22–3.
9 *New Statesman and Nation* (14 July 1945), p. 17.
10 G. Winn, 'Notes on Holland', *New Statesman and Nation*, 6 October 1945), p. 226.

11 M. Livi-Bacci, *Population and Nutrition* (Cambridge, 1990), p. 45.

12 K. Martin, 'Norwegian Holiday', *New Statesman and Nation*
(29 September 1945), p. 210.

13 A. C. Mierzejewski, *The Collapse of the German War Economy, 1944–1945*
(Chapel Hill, NC, 1988), pp. 81–3.

14 The Dean of St Pauls, 'Conversations with Germans', *The Spectator*,
28 December 1945, pp. 613–14.

15 A. B. Lane, *I Saw Poland Betrayed: An American Ambassador Reports to the
American People* (New York, 1948), p. 159.

16 L. Dudley Stamp, 'Land Utilization in Britain', *Geographical Review*,
XXXIII (October 1943), pp. 523–44.

17 C. G. Harris, 'The Ruhr Coal Mining District', *Geographical Review*,
XXXVI (April 1946), pp. 194–221; B. R. Mitchell, *International Historical
Statistics: Europe, 1750–1988* (New York, 1998).

18 R. H. S. Crossman, 'Our Job in Germany', *New Statesman and
Nation* (8 September 1945), pp. 156–7; *New Statesman and Nation*
(15 September 1945), p. 170.

19 H. D. Walston, 'Farming in Poland', *The Spectator* (14 December 1945),
p. 562. 'Germany's Food', *The Spectator* (11 January 1946), pp. 30–31.
'Farming in France', *The Spectator* (1 February 1946), pp. 111–12.

20 Jean Gottmann, *A Geography of Europe* (New York, 1969), p. 142.

21 Alan S. Milward, *The Reconstruction of Europe 1945–51* (London, 1984).

22 Mark Harrison (ed.), *The Economics of World War II: Six Great Powers in
Comparison* (Cambridge, 1998), pp. 36–7.

23 'Ivan Hirst', *The Times* (20 March 2000), p. 21.

24 K. M. Jensen, ed., *Origins of the Cold War: The Novikov, Kennan, and
Roberts 'Long Telegrams' of 1946* (Washington, DC, 1993).

25 Martin Gilbert, *'Never Despair': Winston S. Churchill, 1945–65* (London,
1988), pp. 197–203.

26 Dean Acheson, *Present at the Creation* (New York, 1969), p. 291; A. H.
Vandenberg, Jr, *The Private Papers of Senator Vandenberg* (Boston, MA,
1952), pp. 338–9.

27 X [George F. Kennan], 'The Sources of Soviet Conduct', *Foreign Affairs*,
XXV (July 1947), pp. 566–82.

28 *Ibid.*, p. 581.

29 *Ibid.*, p. 580.

30 Walter Lippmann, *The Cold War: A Study in US Foreign Policy* (New York,
1947), pp. 18–29.

31 *Ibid.*, p. 24.

32 Martin Walker, *The Cold War* (New York, 1994), p. 51.

33 A. W. Dulles, *The Marshall Plan* (Oxford, 1993), pp. 24–7, originally
published 1948.

34 Alan Bullock, *Ernest Bevin: Foreign Secretary 1945–1951* (New York,
1983), p. 422.

35 Walker, *The Cold War*, p. 52.

36 M. J. Hogan, *The Marshall Plan: America, Britain, and the Reconstruction of
Western Europe, 1947–1952* (New York, 1987), p. 3.

37 *Annual Register, 1947*, vol. CLXXXIX (London, 1948), pp. 516–20.

38 W. D. Miscamble, *George F. Kennan and the Making of American Foreign Policy 1947–1950* (Princeton, NJ, 1992), pp. 113–40.

39 John L. Gaddis, *Strategies of Containment* (New York, 1982), pp. 89–109.

40 *Ibid.*, pp. 152–3.

41 F. Ninkovich, *Modernity and Power: A History of the Domino Theory in the Twentieth Century* (Chicago, 1994).

42 Paul Kennedy, *The Rise and Fall of Great Powers* (New York, 1987).

43 Colin S. Gray, *The Geopolitics of Super Power* (Lexington, KY, 1988).

44 Jules Verne, *Around the World in Eighty Days and Five Weeks in a Balloon* (London, 1994), originally published 1873.

45 H. G. Wells, *Anticipations of the Reaction of Mechanical and Scientific Progress upon Human Life and Thought* (London, 1902).

46 Peter Marsh, *Bargaining on Europe: Britain and the First Common Market* (New Haven, CT, 1999), p. 3.

47 Jack Snyder, *Myths of Empire: Domestic Politics and International Ambition* (Ithaca, NY, 1993), pp. 70–72.

48 Andrew Marrison, *British Business and Protection, 1903–1932* (Oxford, 1996).

49 A. T. Mahan, *The Problem of Asia and its Effect upon International Policies* (Boston, MA, 1900), p. 191.

50 J. D. B. Miller, 'Norman Angel and Rationality in International Relations', in Long and Wilson, eds, *Thinkers of the Twenty Year Crisis*, pp. 100–21.

51 Mahan, *Problem of Asia*, p. 129.

8 GLOBALIZATION AND THE DEATH OF GEOPOLITICS?

1 Neil Smith, 'British Loan', in John O'Loughlin, *Dictionary of Geopolitics* (Westport, CT, 1994), p. 30.

2 David S. McLellan, *Dean Acheson: The State Department Years* (New York, 1976), pp. 242–3; John Lamberton Harper, *American Visions of Europe: Franklin D. Roosevelt, George F. Kennan and Dean G. Acheson* (Cambridge, 1994), p. 287.

3 *Harry S. Truman: Containing the Public Messages, Speeches, and Statements of the President, January 1st to December 31st, 1947* (Washington, DC, 1963), pp. 167–72.

4 Alan S. Milward, *Reconstruction of Europe 1945–51* (London, 1984), pp. 242–6; Geoffrey Warner, 'Ernest Bevin and British Foreign Policy, 1945–1951', in Gordon A. Craig and Francis L. Loewenheim, *The Diplomats, 1939–1979* (Princeton, NJ, 1994), pp. 111–12.

5 Carl Strikwerda, 'The Troubled Origins of European Economic Integration: International Iron and Steel and Labor Migration in the Era of World War I', *American Historical Review*, XCVIII/4 (1993), pp. 1106–29.

6 Carolyn Woods Eisenberg, *Drawing the Line: The American Decision to Divide Germany* (New York, 1996), p. 35.

7 Henry Morgenthau, *Germany Is Our Problem* (New York, 1945).

8 A. W. DePorte, *De Gaulle's Foreign Policy 1944–1946* (Cambridge, MA,

1968), pp. 260–9; Milward, *Reconstruction*, p. 128; John W. Young, *Britain and European Unity 1945–1992* (New York, 1993), pp. 7–8.

9 Henry L. Mason, *The European Coal and Steel Community: Experiment in Supranationalism* (The Hague, 1955), pp. 1–9.

10 Edmund Dell, *The Schuman Plan and the British Abdication of Leadership in Europe* (New York, 1995), p. 14; Irwin M. Wall, 'Jean Monnet, the United States and the French Economic Plan', in Douglas Brinkley and Clifford Hackett, eds, *Jean Monnet: The Path the European Unity* (London, 1991), pp. 86–113.

11 Dean Acheson, *Present at the Creation: My Years at the State Department* (New York, 1969), pp. 31–2.

12 Phil Gramm, 'There's No Need to Go It Alone', *Daily Telegraph* (16 May 2000), p. 22.

13 Walter Lippmann, *Western Unity and the Common Market* (London, 1962), p. 3.

14 Graeme Donald Snooks, *Global Transition: A General Theory of Economic Development* (London, 1999), p. 17.

15 Eddy Lee, *The Asian Financial Crisis: The Challenge for Social Policy* (Geneva, 1998).

16 George Soros, *The Crisis of Global Capitalism* (New York, 1998), p. xxiii.

17 D. J. Markwell, 'J. M. Keynes, Idealism, and the Economic Bases of Peace', in David Long and Peter Wilson, eds, *Thinkers of the Twenty Years' Crisis: Inter-war Idealism Reassessed* (Oxford, 1995), pp. 206–8.

18 Peter J. Hugill, *Global Communications since 1844: Geopolitics and Technology* (Baltimore, MD, 1999). See also *World Trade since 1431: Geography, Technology and Capitalism* (Baltimore, MD, 1993).

19 Simon Reich, *The Fruits of Fascism: Postwar Prosperity in Historical Perspective* (Ithaca, NY, 1990).

20 Samuel P. Huntington, *The Clash of Civilizations and the Remaking of World Order* (New York, 1996).

21 B. R. Mitchell, *International Historical Statistics: The Americas, 1750–1993* (New York, 1998), 4th edn, pp. 479–80.

22 Thomas J. Christensen, 'Chinese Realpolitík', *Foreign Affairs*, LXXV/5 (1996), pp. 37–52; Brad Roberts, Robert A. Manning and Ronald N. Montaperto, 'China: The Forgotten Nuclear Power', *Foreign Affairs*, LXXIX/4 (2000), pp. 53–63.

23 Niall Ferguson, *Paper and Iron: Hamburg Business and German Politics in the Era of Inflation, 1897–1927* (Cambridge, 1995), pp. 32–4; Jack Snyder, *Myths of Empire: Domestic Politics and International Ambition* (Ithaca, NY, 1993), pp. 71–3.

24 Peter Gourevitch, *Politics in Hard Times: Comparative Responses to International Economic Crises* (Ithaca, NY, 1986), pp. 147–53.

Select Bibliography

Agnew, John, *Geopolitics: Revisioning World Politics* (London, 1998)

Blouet, B. W., *Halford Mackinder: A Biography* (College Station, TX, 1987)

Boog, Horst, *et al.*, *Germany and the Second World War: Volume IV: The Attack on the Soviet Union* (Oxford, 1998)

Brinkley, Douglas and David R. Facey-Crowther, eds, *The Atlantic Charter* (London, 1994)

Brzezinski, Zbigniew, *The Grand Chessboard: American Primacy and Its Geostrategic Imperatives* (New York, 1997)

Coudenhove-Kalergi, Count Richard N., *The Totalitarian State against Man* (London, 1938)

Dell, Edmund, *The Schuman Plan and the British Abdication of Leadership in Europe* (Oxford, 1995)

DePorte, A. W., *De Gaulle's Foreign Policy 1944–1946* (Cambridge, MA, 1968)

Dodds, Klaus, *Geopolitics in a Changing World* (Harlow, 2000)

—, and David Atkinson, eds, *Geopolitical Traditions: A Century of Geopolitical Thought* (London and New York, 2000)

Doyle, Michael W., and G. John Ikenberry, *New Thinking in International Relations Theory* (Boulder, CO, 1997)

Eisenberg, Carolyn Woods, *Drawing the Line: The American Decision to Divide Germany, 1944–1949* (Cambridge, 1996)

Ferguson, Niall, *The Pity of War* (London, 1998)

Fischer, Fritz, *Germany's Aims in the First World War* (New York, 1967)

Gaddis, John L., *Strategies of Containment* (New York, 1982)

Gilbert, Martin, ed., *Winston Churchill and Emery Reves: Correspondence, 1937–1964* (Austin, TX, 1997)

Goda, Norman J. W., *Tomorrow the World: Hitler, Northwest Africa, and the Path toward America* (College Station, TX, 1998)

Haggman, Bertil, 'Rudolf Kjellén and Modern Swedish Geopolitics', *Geopolitics*, vol. III, no. 2, 1998, pp. 99–112

Harper, John Lamberton, *American Visions of Europe: Franklin D. Roosevelt, George F. Kennan and Dean G. Acheson* (Cambridge, 1994)

Harrison, Mark, *Accounting for War: Soviet Production, Employment and*

195

the Defence Burden 1940–1945 (Cambridge, 1996)

—, *The Economics of World War II: Six Great Powers in Comparison* (Cambridge, 1998)

Hearden, Patrick J., *Roosevelt Confronts Hitler: America's Entry into World War II* (DeKalb, IL, 1987)

Heater, Derek, *The Idea of European Unity* (New York, 1992)

Heffernan, Michael, *The Meaning of Europe* (New York, 1998)

Held, David, Anthony McGrew, David Goldblatt and Jonathan Perraton, *Global Transformations: Politics, Economics and Culture* (Cambridge, 2000)

Herwig, Holger H., 'Geopolitik: Haushofer, Hitler and Lebensraum', in Colin S. Gray and Geoffrey Sloan, eds, *Geopolitics, Geography and Strategy* (London, 1999), pp. 218–41

Heske, Henning, 'Karl Haushofer: His Role in German Geopolitics and in Nazi Politics', *Political Geography Quarterly*, 6 (1987), pp. 135–44

—, and Rolf Wesche, 'Karl Haushofer 1869–1946', *Geographers: Biobibliographical Studies*, 12 (1988), pp. 95–106

Hodgson, Godfrey, *The Colonel: The Life and Wars of Henry Stimson, 1867–1950* (New York, 1990)

Holdar, Sven, 'The Ideal State and the Power of Geography: The Life-Work of Rudolf Kjellén', *Political Geography*, vol. II, no. 2 (1992), pp. 307–23

Hooson, David J. M., *A New Soviet Heartland?* (Princeton, NJ, 1964)

Hugill, Peter J., *Global Communications since 1844: Geopolitics and Technology* (Baltimore, MD, 1999)

—, *World Trade since 1431: Geography, Technology, and Capitalism* (Baltimore, MD, 1993)

Jäckel, Eberhard, *Hitler's World View: A Blueprint for Power* (Cambridge, MA, 1981)

Jensen, Kenneth M., ed., *Origins of the Cold War: The Novikov, Kennan, and Roberts 'Long Telegrams' of 1946* (Washington, DC, 1993)

Kennedy, Paul M., *The Rise of the Anglo-German Antagonism 1860–1914* (London, 1980)

Kimball, Warren F., *Swords or Ploughshares? The Morgenthau Plan for Defeated Nazi Germany, 1943–46* (New York, 1976)

Kissinger, Henry, *Diplomacy* (New York, 1994)

Kleinschmidt, Harald, *The Nemesis of Power* (London, 2000)

Lippmann, Walter, *US Foreign Policy: Shield of the Republic* (Boston, MA, 1943)

Mackinder, H. J., *Democratic Ideals and Reality: A Study in the Politics of Reconstruction* (London, 1919)

McDougall, Walter A., *France's Rhineland Diplomacy, 1914–1924: The Last Bid for Balance of Power in Europe* (Princeton, NJ, 1978)

Milward, Alan S., *The Fascist Economy of Norway* (Oxford, 1972)

—, *The Reconstruction of Europe 1945–51* (London, 1984)

—, *War, Economy and Society 1939–1945* (Berkeley and Los Angeles, CA, 1977)

Morgenthau, Jr, Henry, *Germany Is Our Problem* (New York, 1945)

Murphy, David T., *The Heroic Earth: Geopolitical Thought in Weimar Germany, 1918–1933* (Kent, OH, 1997)

O'Loughlin, John, ed., *Dictionary of Geopolitics* (Westport, CT, 1994)

—, and van der Wusten, H., 'The Political Geography of Panregions', *Geographical Review* 80, 1–20 (1990)

Overy, Richard, *Russia's War* (London, 1999)

—, *War and Economy in the Third Reich* (Oxford, 1994)

—, *Why the Allies Won* (New York, 1995)

Parker, Geoffrey, *Geopolitics: Past, Present and Future* (London, 1998)

Parker, W. H., *Mackinder: Geography as an Aid to Statecraft* (Oxford, 1982)

Reich, Simon, *Fruits of Fascism: Postwar Prosperity in Historical Perspective* (Ithaca, NY, 1990)

Rosecrance, Richard, *The Rise of the Trading State: Commerce and Conquest in the Modern World* (New York, 1986)

Schweller, Randall L., *Deadly Imbalances: Tripolarity and Hitler's Strategy of World Conquest* (New York, 1998)

Snyder, Jack, *Myths of Empire: Domestic Politics and International Ambition* (Ithaca, NY, 1991)

Spykman, N. J., *America's Strategy in World Politics: The United States and the Balance of Power* (New York, 1942)

Stoakes, Geoffrey, *Hitler and the Quest for World Dominion* (New York, 1986)

Taylor, Peter J., *The Way the Modern World Works: World Hegemony to World Impasse* (Chichester, 1996)

Tuathail, Gearóid Ó., Simon Dalby and Paul Routledge, eds, *The Geopolitics Reader* (London, 1998)

Whittlesey, Derwent, Charles Colby and Richard Hartshorne, *German Strategy for World Conquest* (New York, 1942)

Photographic Acknowledgements

The authors and publishers wish to express their thanks to the below sources of illustrative material and/or permission to reproduce it. (The remaining illustrative material is courtesy of the author.)

"All Gaul Is United Into One Part": cartoon of De Gaulle's face in the map of France, 1961, Special Collections, College of William and Mary, Williamsburg, VA.

Cartoons by Dr Seuss, University of California, San Diego, Mandeville Special Collections Library (Dr. Seuss Collection).

Index